Praise for
Secrets of Millionaire Moms

*"Tamara gives the equivalent of an MBA in digest form
for women entrepreneurs! Her choice of subjects provides
true life 'case studies' that demonstrate what it takes
to succeed in business while having balance in life and the
ability to create good will and generosity of spirit in sisterhood.
Tamara is a true asset that deserves recognition
for being a wonderful role model herself!"*

—BARBARA J. FRIEDMAN, PRESIDENT OF LICENSING,
LIZ CLAIBORNE, INC

*"Every woman should use this book as her guide
to starting and growing a business—even if she isn't a 'mom.'
The book inspires you to great vision and then gives you
the practical, day-to-day advice on how to turn
that vision into reality. Plus it is the first book
I have read that deals realistically with the challenges
of combining family and business opportunities."*

—SHARON G. HADARY, EXECUTIVE DIRECTOR,
CENTER FOR WOMEN'S BUSINESS RESEARCH

*"Tamara has magnificently blended inspirational real-life
stories from remarkable women with critical business skills
such as creative marketing and fund raising.
I repeatedly caught myself reading ahead to see what came next."*

—JULIE GARELLA, DIRECTOR OF CLIENT DEVELOPMENT,
CITIGROUP CAPITAL STRATEGIES

**Also by
Tamara Monosoff**

*The Mom Inventors Handbook:
How to Turn Your Great Idea into the Next Big Thing*

SECRETS *of* MILLIONAIRE MOMS

LEARN HOW THEY TURNED GREAT IDEAS INTO BOOMING BUSINESSES— AND HOW YOU CAN TOO!

TAMARA MONOSOFF

McGraw-Hill

New York   Chicago   San Francisco   Lisbon   London   Madrid
Mexico City   Milan   New Delhi   San Juan   Seoul
Singapore   Sydney   Toronto

ISBN-13: 978-0-07-147892-2
ISBN-10: 0-07-147892-2

To my husband and dearest friend,
Brad,
and to our precious daughters,
Sophia Colette
and
Kiara Lauren

Contents

Acknowledgments

The success of this project has been dependent on the wisdom, support, talent, and commitment of many people, on both a personal and professional level, to whom I am deeply indebted.

The impetus for writing this book came from the overwhelming response of thousands of women who are part of our www.mom inventors.com community, as well as women everywhere who seek to create better lives for themselves and their families.

That is why I wish to express my deepest appreciation and gratitude to the extraordinary women profiled in this book. Not only did they offer their precious time, but while doing so, they shared their wisdom, knowledge, and struggles in transforming their dreams into thriving businesses. Their contributions were truly gifts from the heart . . . for everyone's benefit.

Once again, my family has proved to be an unceasing, continuous resource of love and support. My mother and father, Geraldine and Harris Monosoff, continue to be my inspiration and guiding angels—words fail to describe what they mean to me.

Through her endless generosity, my sister Dana redefines the meaning of "support." Each of my siblings and their spouses has instantly stepped forward when I needed them most. Scott and Tia each offered valuable comments on drafts. I am especially grateful to Christopher Dworin, whose detailed comments improved every chapter of this book.

My husband's parents, David and Ginny Kofoed, have also been present with love, support, and frequent child care! They often leave their own interests and lives behind to support my work.

I thank Juley Peterson, who's on my staff, for her willingness to assume ever-greater responsibility at Mom Inventors, Inc. while I wrote this book.

I am grateful for the dedicated and talented team at McGraw-Hill—David Dell'Accio, Tom Lau, Daina Penikas, and Lizz Aviles—and I especially want to express my appreciation to Donya Dickerson for her superior editorial guidance

I wish to acknowledge Jessica Faust (my literary agent) who is setting a new standard in her field for effectiveness and commitment to her clients.

My editor and friend, Jennifer Rung, has stood by my side throughout this project and has the phenomenal ability to improve the words of everything that she touches all while juggling the roles of mom and entrepreneur in her own right.

I must also thank a new friend, Shari Santos, who meticulously transcribed hours of interviews, adding her own enthusiasm to the project.

Linda Davey, Nell Merlino, and Randy Williams each provided expert knowledge and content which improved this book.

I wish to thank three extraordinary women, all leaders in their respective fields: Barbara J. Friedman, President of Licensing, Liz Claiborne, Inc.; Sharon G. Hadary, Executive Director, Center for Women's Business Research; and Julie Garella, Director of Client Development, Citigroup Capital Strategies, for taking the time to share their insights and thoughts about this book.

Greg Carson has been a wonderful mentor in terms of understanding "the numbers" for my business, as well as helping to ensure the accuracy of the financial sections of this book. I appreciate his clarity and kindness in teaching me to overcome my fear of "the numbers."

Jim McClaskey, my CPA, was enormously generous in sharing his expert comments on "the numbers" sections in this book.

I am indebted to Ann Noder for her passion and enthusiasm.

And most importantly, there are few words that adequately describe my appreciation for my husband Brad, who has spent endless hours listening, brainstorming, and supporting this project as well as sharing the care for our daughters.

Introduction

When I was first contemplating this book, I wrestled with what kind of subject matter I wanted to share. Should I write a business book, sharing what I have learned from my own experiences as an entrepreneur—disclosing mistakes and tough lessons learned? Or should I write a book that shares the stories and life profiles of many of the women I have come to admire—women who have guided me both directly and by example?

Each model had elements I thought would be beneficial to other women who want to start or grow their own business. And as you'll see, I chose to write a book that strives to do both.

First, I identified a number of key business concepts that I believe are important and which, based on my frequent communication with women entrepreneurs, present the greatest challenges. Next, I identified 17 extraordinary women who, based on their own success and experience, could help explain these core concepts, and at the same time offer inspiration. They are some of the most successful entrepreneurs of our day, with businesses ranging from retail to manufacturing to public relations. These are not women who have ascended the corporate ladder to reach the CEO level (a significant but very different kind of achievement). Rather, each of them had an idea that they developed, some quite literally from their kitchen tables, and grew them into multi-million dollar companies; ranging from $5 million to $350 million so far.

I chose to feature mothers in particular for this book. I wanted to provide examples of women from several generations who figured out how to love and care for their families while turning their passions and personal needs into ways to create financial freedom. The unexpected gift many of them share is that their wealth has provided them a vehicle to give to others at a level that they never imagined possible.

In this book you'll find many of their "secrets": their high points, their low points, their personal histories, and most of all, their business methods which I hope you will find intriguing. I wanted to pass along the best of what they shared with me.

This information ranges from goal-setting and understanding financials to achieving life balance and overcoming adversity of many kinds. It's all meant to provide inspiration *and* information to help get you started—or get to the next level—in your own endeavor, million-dollar or otherwise! My aim is to show, rather than tell, you how to follow in the footsteps of these remarkable women.

A PERSONAL ODYSSEY

Meeting and speaking with each of these phenomenal businesswomen has been among the most rewarding things I have done in my career. In fact, the evening after each interview I often found myself unable to sleep, replaying our conversations again and again in my mind. And my feelings were consistently reaffirmed by Shari, my transcriptionist, who would return the interviews with comments such as, "Awesome!"

I learned that none of these women started out with any obvious advantage. And none of them were handed their success. In fact, most have overcome tremendous odds, including obstacles that many would consider debilitating, if not insurmountable. What they all share is a tenacious work ethic, optimism about life's possibilities, and a generosity of spirit. And though none of these women seem to have approached their business endeavors with an expectation that anyone would give them anything, they each now are consistently generous to others.

My interviews often exceeded the time I had requested—and often required follow-up communication to clarify or augment answers. Nevertheless, each of these women graciously extended themselves out of a desire to support this project. Further, I found their interviews to be a double gift: not only did they provide unbelievably rich insights for this book but they also provided inspiration and knowledge that have helped me with my own business. After each interview, I found myself rethinking my own business methods based on the new concepts I'd learned.

Since these women are so interesting and inspiring, I have attempted to go beyond the basic business aspects I had initially intended to explore. I asked them to share those things that made the critical difference in their extraordinary achievements, and to share their inspirations.

To say I am grateful, fails to reflect my appreciation for each of them adequately.

Throughout this book I have included many direct excerpts from my conversations with these women, as well as interviews with other selected experts, because I am confident that you will relish their words and their experiences as much as I do. I also hope that as you read the success secrets of the 17 women in this book, you'll develop your own understanding of the business fundamentals I consider keys to entrepreneurial success.

WHAT YOU'LL DISCOVER

As a mom and entrepreneur myself, I wanted to share the information as I have experienced it: as a complex process inextricably linked with my personal life. As a result, each chapter in this book includes both personal and business information. There are four chapters that focus on issues around entrepreneurship at a personal level. The first chapter, in particular, discusses the history of women's ambivalence toward money and techniques for dealing with it. Then in Chapter 5, I examine challenges and myths around the endless struggle for life "balance." In Chapter 7, I share how these successful women have found the strength to do what they've done, often in the face of enormous adversity. And in Chapter 8, I provide a framework that I hope will help you see what it really takes to create the life you desire.

Using stories, personal experiences, and dialogue, my goal is to reveal information, rather than to lecture about it. Chapters 2, 3, 4, and 6 focus directly on several key business requirements, including developing a business plan, using creative marketing and structuring the business, raising money, and understanding "the numbers."

Most importantly, the insights each of these remarkable women shared are interspersed among the chapters. Each chapter includes the personal profiles of two of them. All are entrepreneurs and all but one are moms; the sole exception being Maxine Clark of Build-A-Bear Workshop, whose brilliance and wisdom make her the honorary mom here . . . as well as to the children she serves (including my own daughters, who love their "furry friends"). The women I interviewed are

- **Madelyn Alfano**, owner of Maria's Italian Kitchen (www.mariasitaliankitchen.com)
- **Rachel Ashwell**, founder of Shabby Chic, author, and designer (www.shabbychic.com)
- **Karen Belasco**, founder of Good Fortunes Cookie Company (www.goodfortunes.com)
- **Jeanne Bice**, founder of The Quacker Factory and QVC sensation (www.quackerfactory.com)
- **Julie Clark**, founder of the Baby Einstein Company and currently The Safe Side (www.thesafeside.com)
- **Maxine Clark**, founder and chief executive bear of Build-A-Bear Workshop (www.buildabearworkshop.com)
- **Debi Davis**, founder of Fit America MD (www.fitamericamd.com)
- **Tomima Edmark**, inventor of TopsyTail and currently founder of HerRoom (www.HerRoom.com) and HisRoom (www.HisRoom.com)
- **Teri Gault**, founder of The Grocery Game (www.TheGroceryGame.com)
- **Kathy Gendel**, founder of Breezies Intimates and QVC sensation (www.qvc.com)
- **Victoria Knight-McDowell**, founder of Airborne Health (www.airbornehealth.com)

- **Mary Micucci**, founder of Along Came Mary Productions (www.alongcamemary.com)
- **Deann Murphy**, founder of Distlefink Designs Inc. and currently Craft Clicks
- **Lane Nemeth**, founder of Discovery Toys and currently Petlane (www.Petlane.com)
- **Maria de Lourdes Sobrino**, founder of Lulu's Dessert (www.lulusdessert.com)
- **Lillian Vernon**, founder of Lillian Vernon Corporation (www.lillianvernon.com)
- **Terrie M. Williams**, president and founder of The Terrie Williams Agency, founder of the Stay Strong Foundation, and author (www.terriewilliams.com and www.thestaystrong foundation.org)

Because I have learned and been inspired so much by these women myself, I am certain that you will find their experience valuable too. So whether you picked up this book because you are seeking to start or grow your own business, because you want to be inspired, or because you are simply interested in the lives of 17 extraordinary women who've made it big, I believe you will find your time well spent in the pages to follow.

The Fear Factor:
Overcoming Anxiety
about Money,
Failure, and Success

THE FEAR FACTOR: MONEY AND SUCCESS

Like it or not, fear is a motivating factor in all our lives. In some ways it's incredibly healthy—it prevents us from driving too fast or stepping too close to the edge of a cliff. In other ways, though, it can inhibit us from doing things that can benefit us . . . and those around us. It can even prevent us from pursuing our dreams. It's these latter fears that I will talk about in this chapter—specifically as they relate to women, money, and success.

Many women who consider starting their own business encounter unexpected mental roadblocks that prevent them from moving forward. Many times, these roadblocks are unconscious. In other words, we're not exactly sure what's stopping us . . . but there's an unexplained internal brake light that goes on again and again, often without obvious explanation. One brake light is often related to money.

The fear of finding/borrowing money, handling money—even making money—is often powerful and debilitating, holding us back from our dreams. As I interviewed the 17 successful entrepreneurs for this book, I realized how much more common these fears are for women than men, almost certainly due to the socialization of women and money throughout history, and due to residual attitudes that remain to this day. It's been a barrier for me, for instance, partially rooted in both my own discomfort with math and because of a lack of practical education in how math relates to money and generating wealth. Why do we learn so much in high school about algebra, geometry, and trigonometry and virtually nothing about budgeting, investing, and economics?

My experience was echoed throughout the process of interviewing the women for this book. Even after creating multi-million dollar enterprises, many of them confessed they still hadn't overcome their fear of—or resistance to—learning "the numbers." Others recall the moment when they simply had to get over it, even if they didn't really want to! Perhaps that's why Lillian Vernon, founder of the incredibly successful Lillian Vernon catalogs, asked me, "Shouldn't the discussion of money be your first chapter?" I agreed with her, so here we are.

This chapter breaks down the many fears women have when considering entrepreneurship—most of which relate directly or indirectly to money. Whether the fears are of failure or of success, most are rooted in women's attitudes about money.

FEAR OF MONEY

Why is facing the fear of money so important? Because money is what drives your business. And money is what creates possibilities for you once you accomplish your goals—possibilities for giving to yourself, to your family, and to the world at large. And giving, in my experience, is a subject women seldom fear! Money is one vehicle that in the end, allows us to create and give on a grander scale than ever before.

When it comes to money, it's no mystery why many women are uncomfortable with the topic. Factors like social history, child-raising methods, gender roles, and expectations of femininity—in addition to a lack of role models and very real institutional barriers—make it clear why so many of us are still in the dark when it comes to making and managing money.

And although subjects such as science and math are being taught to girls in school, curriculums rarely include the business elements of making money. Girls in particular, traditionally are not encouraged by schools or at home to focus on how they will earn money to support themselves. Even though we pride ourselves on how far we have come to equalize gender roles, as a culture, the traditional roles we play as men and women still prevail.

WOMEN AND MONEY: TODAY'S ISSUES

In *Money, A Memoir*, Liz Perle says, "there are strong gender differences when it comes to money—differences of identity and of historical roles. For men, the interplay of money and love and power has not really changed in thousands of years; they have always been the providers, and their identities and power come from this old survival-based role."

Even in business, many women are initially motivated by factors other than money. For Julie Clark, money has been the by-product of starting a business. She founded her first company, Baby Einstein, in order to provide educational videos for her own babies. Her newest venture, The Safe Side, produces products that help keep kids safe from strangers and child predators.

"I didn't start Baby Einstein or The Safe Side because I felt like I was going to make a million dollars," says Julie. "I really started them because they were something that I loved and wanted to do."

She nevertheless grew Baby Einstein into a multi-million dollar business, which she sold to The Walt Disney Company. And that gave her the funds to launch The Safe Side (www.thesafeside.com).

When asked about whether she talked about money before starting her business, Terrie Williams, best-selling author and president &

founder of the Terrie M. Williams Agency said, " . . . my goal in life was just to make a difference, to serve humanity, and I would often-times, until my business partner and I connected, just really lose sight of that." She remembered discussing with her partner a price quote for a prospective client in the early days, " . . . I'm embarrassed to tell you this, but I wanted to say, 'I was thinking somewhere along the line of ten grand a month, right?' He said, 'No! We're going to ask for fifty.' . . . my mouth dropped. But do you know that we got it?"

I recall a woman inventor whom we were helping to negotiate a licensing contract with another company, as she contemplated what she hoped to get out of the deal. She framed her expectations by say-ing, "I don't need to eat lobster every night." My husband's response was "Okay, let's get the best deal we can and *I'll* eat the lobster." This, to me, was a telling example of the comfort level and socialization of women versus men when it comes to acquiring money.

MILLION-DOLLAR SECRET

Women are prone to undervalue themselves in the business world. They shouldn't be shy about commanding higher fees or prices, says Terrie Williams.

"There are hair stylists and makeup artists who get five grand a day for an hour of work. It is what you say it is. We really have to learn to ask for what we're worth. And the market (value of your offer) is what you say it is," Terrie explains.

In addition, "Women have been socialized to think a lot more about spending money than making money," says Nell Merlino, founder of Count Me In for Women's Economic Independence (www.count-me-in.org), an organization that supports women launching small businesses by giving them micro loans. "I have been surprised at the level of fear and reluctance around money," continues

Nell. "There's some real confusion about what it means to be rich." For most of us, our first female role model is our mother. And most of our mothers were well into adulthood before the first real gains in higher education and career advancement for women in the 20th century were made, so they themselves weren't comfortable with money.

Fortunately, there are now women's groups like Count Me In that exist specifically to provide business and financial role models and support for women. And in recent years, many business schools have sought to expand women's enrollment (now about 30 percent) dramatically.

LINGERING INSTITUTIONAL BARRIERS

Before women entered and proved themselves in entrepreneurial ventures, banks and other financial institutions had little incentive to cater to women borrowers. In the 1970s my mother was in the business of fixing up and selling homes. I remember her anger when she was unable to qualify for a home loan without "her husband's" signature.

Only very recently have banks begun actively seeking to fund women-owned businesses. They should be more forthcoming—the market is certainly financially attractive. According to the Center for Women's Business Research (www.womensbusinessresearch.org), "today nearly 10.4 million U.S. firms are 50 percent or more women-owned, employing more than 12.8 million people, and generating nearly $1.9 trillion in sales." The statistics speak for themselves—and they're telling banks that women-owned businesses represent a substantial opportunity for revenue growth.

That banks recognize this is new indeed; many—if not most—of the women featured in this book didn't have much luck with traditional lending institutions when building their businesses. However, statistics show that women-owned businesses are just as financially strong and creditworthy as the average firm, and are just as likely to remain in business.

As recently as 1985, Madelyn Alfano of Maria's Italian Kitchen couldn't get traditional financing. "I opened my first restaurant for less than $25,000," she explained. "At age 28, as a woman, and in the restaurant business, I had three strikes against me. I got credit from a restaurant fixture place—because the guy trusted me—the banks wouldn't give me any money."

On a positive note, a dramatic shift is occurring as banks and other financial institutions recognize that women business owners represent a source of substantial revenue and influence. Statistics show that women who obtain capital to expand their businesses and set specific expansion goals succeed in achieving or exceeding their goals (Center for Women's Business Research, 2006). In other words, women are a great investment. With momentum on our side, it's up to us to take steps to overcome our own personal fear of money—we are up to the task!

OVERCOMING OUR FEAR OF MONEY

Our financial fears can be a huge barrier to success. Believing that it will be impossible to get the money to fund your business, and/or that it will be too challenging to manage your money once you succeed, can be overwhelming and among the biggest obstacles you will have to overcome.

There are other fears, as well—conscious and unconscious—when it comes to starting your own business. This section outlines these fears, examines how realistic they are, and provides methods to accept and overcome them.

In my experience, most people's fear and insecurity is rooted in either the fear of failure . . . or the fear of success. Both of these are valid. But both can be overcome.

FEAR OF FINANCIAL CONSEQUENCES

The Issues

There are other aspects to failure that cannot be overlooked—the potential for very real negative financial consequences—both for yourself and for your business. On the personal side, a failed business means that you're out of a job and that you risk losing any collateral you've put up for the business, such as your home. (And finding a new job can be surprisingly challenging for someone accustomed to being an entrepreneur.)

Debi Davis is open about the fact that she had gone bankrupt with a jewelry business before starting her current company, FitAmerica MD. Before she started her successful company that provides nutriceutical supplements to aid in weight loss, she felt a great deal of distress about her situation. "I was unemployable because I had been entrepreneurial," she says. "I'd had businesses before or worked with my husband, so even though I was incredibly qualified, people were afraid to hire me because they didn't think I would stick around."

Other personal consequences of financial failure could include a compromised credit rating, overdue credit card payments, and lingering debts to friends and family . . . which can make facing those family get-togethers a little awkward!

On the business side, potential financial failure forces you to consider many things. One of them may be your reputation. If you go out of business without paying your vendors, you could bring your vendors down with you (some are likely to be small businesses too). You may feel responsible for your employees, who would be depending on their jobs to support their families. And if your business fails, you may have a hard time getting funding again. The complexity of your considerations increases with the size of the business—it's not just about you anymore.

Even when you reach a certain level of success, and even if you're personally financially secure, financial fear may remain . . . but with different motivating factors. Instead of worrying about your mortgage payment, for instance, you'll face more complex financial issues such as meeting payroll (i.e., other people's mortgages!) and the need to raise capital to market and grow the company. Understanding that these demands and more are a part of business is the key to taking on your fear and gaining control.

How to Deal with the Fear of Financial Failure

First, understand that anything worth attaining takes some risk . . . and risk underlies all entrepreneurial endeavors.

However, there are methods to temper your risk, and you can retain a certain comfort level either by creating a safety net or by moving slowly enough that the business can support itself as it grows.

Debi advises women starting off to proceed with financial caution . . . and explains that if you're consumed with how you're going to pay this month's rent, it's tough to focus on your business. "Make sure you have your basic home nut covered for a chunk of time," she says. "In other words, if you know your business isn't going to make money for six months, you need to have enough money set aside to pay your bills and feed your family without having to worry."

Teri Gault, who started The Grocery Game (www.thegro-cerygame.com) with absolutely nothing in the bank, found that grow-ing "organically" helped her find success. She started her company, which provides subscribers with weekly information on rock-bottom grocery sales and instructions on how to maximize "couponing," with-out ever taking on loans, and grew by re-investing all the money she made into the business.

Shabby Chic's founder, Rachel Ashwell, talks about the pros and cons of loans.

"I'm not really big on borrowing money. It may be to my detri-ment to live within my means . . . it may be a missed opportunity," says Ashwell. "But I was always very aware that there's only so much pressure you should put on yourself."

Lane Nemeth of Discovery Toys—and now, Petlane (www.pet-lane.com)—took a different tack to handling the pressure and finan-cial fear. After borrowing $50,000 from her brother-in-law to fund Discovery Toys, her first business, she said, "I took the fear, external-ized it, put it in a box, and removed it from myself. I said, 'I'm not going to fail.'"

Her strategy worked. She grew Discovery Toys into a $100+ mil-lion business before selling it.

Rachel Ashwell

Rachel Ashwell is a woman who could have given in to fear.

Not only did she leave school at 16, but in her twenties she became separated from her husband. At that time, she had two babies under the age of 2.

So, in 1989 she took a chance and started her retail business, Shabby Chic. With her babies by her side, she scouted flea markets for items she could refinish, and her pieces became an instant hit in her Santa Monica, California, store. Never did she fathom it would grow as big as it has today.

The Rachel Ashwell® Shabby Chic® brand has since expanded to include slipcover furniture, poplin and linen bedding, baby bedding, home accessories, a television series, and design books. Also, Rachel has a line of home furnishings known as Simply Shabby Chic sold exclusively through Target stores.

She has also introduced Rachel Ashwell® Shabby Chic® Studio—a more affordable line of slipcover furniture sold through retailers nationwide. The line includes adult and baby bedding and home accessories such as lampshades, chair pads, cots/camp stools, and candles that have since debuted to rave reviews.

Rachel has also written five books, including her original design guide, Shabby Chic®. Four more books followed: Shabby Chic's® Treasure Hunting and Decorating Guide, Shabby Chic® Home, Shabby Chic®—The Gift of Giving, and Rachel Ashwell® Shabby Chic® Sumptuous Settings and Other Lovely Things.

In the fall of 1999, "Rachel Ashwell® Shabby Chic ®" premiered on the E! channel and Style network, guiding viewers on how to bring her distinctive look home.

© Photo credit: Edmund Barr

OVERCOME YOUR FEAR WITH KNOWLEDGE

The best way to mitigate your financial risk, however, is by gaining the knowledge and information that will ultimately bring you success. The more good information you gain, the lower your risk.

So where can you get this information and knowledge? School, of course, is the obvious option, but that can be challenging for people who are at home with children or working full-time and trying to start a business. For those entrepreneurs who don't have the luxury of attending school, there are many resources available—specifically, other women. You can find peers through support groups such as NAWBO (National Association of Women Business Owners) or your local Chamber of Commerce. I also recommend finding mentors—women or men—who can support and guide you.

MILLION-DOLLAR SECRET

It's been said that the smartest people know what they don't know. Madelyn Alfano, who built a $19 million restaurant company from scratch, agrees. Her secret?

"You have to educate yourself, and you have to find people who are smarter than you, to help you," says Madelyn. "I always believe in asking for advice from the smart people."

Reading can also be a great source of information and inspiration. Every time I read *Entrepreneur Magazine* I feel re-energized and find great ideas. Other terrific publications include *Inc. Magazine, Fortune*

Small Business, Fast Company, Business 2.0, Fortune, and *Forbes,* not to mention the many free online news sources like www.cnn-money.com.

FEAR OF FAILURE

In addition to the fear of money, there are several other anxieties about starting a business that can get in the way of realizing our dreams, including the fear of failure. This fear is completely natural and easy to understand. Nobody wants to fail . . . and most people feel failure is a personal reflection on their skills, talents, and abilities. Unfortunately, it's the fear of failure that holds so many of us back from trying at all. In my opinion, that translates into a lot of lost potential and underused talent! It is important to remember that most human beings learn and excel through lessons learned from failure. It has been said that Thomas Edison failed thousands of times before he succeeded in inventing the light bulb.

The following are the specific aspects of the fear of failure that I have observed and some ideas about how to get through them.

POTENTIAL FOR EMBARRASSMENT
The Issues
Most people will do just about anything to avoid being embarrassed. And when you start a business, it is often difficult to separate its success or failure from your own sense of self-worth. So it is not uncommon for an entrepreneur to associate a business failure with a personal one.

Other factors that can add to your fear of embarrassment include the potential failure to live up to others' expectations or failure to meet promised obligations. When you ask others for their support, you're asking them, in essence, to place their confidence in you. Thus, a business failure can make you feel that you did not deserve the confidence others had in you. In addition, if your company has been in the media and you have created a public profile, the feelings of embarrassment can be amplified by your visibility and exposure to large numbers of people.

How to Deal with It

Certainly, a failed business is likely to have a direct negative impact on others, such as suppliers and investors. However, a fact of doing business is that every transaction and relationship carries risk, and other businesspeople should be aware of this.

Steve Jobs, the phenomenally successful founder of Apple Computer and Pixar, explained in a commencement address at Stanford University how he has dealt with fear[1]:

> "Remembering that I'll be dead soon is the most important tool I've ever encountered to help me make the big choices in life," said Jobs. "Because almost everything—all external expectations, all pride, all fear of embarrassment or failure— these things just fall away in the face of death, leaving only what is truly important."

If this resonates well with you, use it. Otherwise, find a perspective that diminishes your fear and rely on that to give you courage. I've encountered successful businesspeople who speak of early failures as phenomenal training grounds and badges of honor—badges that grant them the privilege of basking in their ultimate success.

When Debi Davis went bankrupt, for example, she didn't become bogged down with embarrassment of financial failure, but instead took action, eager to apply what she had learned.

According to Debi, once she got back on her feet, "I went back and paid people that I didn't have to pay." By doing so she preserved the relationships and her reputation, and in fact worked with many of the same vendors with the new company. "They were all right there for me," she says.

---

[1] Commencement address reprinted in *Fortune* magazine, September 2005.

THE INSIDE STORY

Debi Davis

Debi Davis is a great example of how to deal with the fears of entrepreneurship. The failure of her first business, which she ran with her husband, forced her to declare bankruptcy. But instead of wallowing in self-pity or fearing a second failure, she pulled herself up by the bootstraps, sold her watch for working capital, and used it to fund what became a $45 million business—FitAmerica.

Faced with a major business obstacle again, years later— her business went from $45 million to $5 million in an hour, due to circumstances beyond her control—Debi once again faced the prospect of failure.

But she reinvented her business yet again. Today, FitAmerica MD provides personal health diagnostics to health clubs and gyms, along with products to help people lose weight and live healthier lives.

For three consecutive years, *Working Woman* magazine recognized Fit America MD as one of America's top 500 women-owned businesses. Debi was awarded Ernst & Young's Entrepreneur of the Year Award in 1999 for health, and has been featured on national TV and in media publications including *Success Magazine, Fortune Small Business,* and *Newsweek.*

Debi is a regular writer for several magazines and newspapers, and has written three books that address weight loss challenges. Her latest work, *Wisdoms for a Better Life*, will be available in early 2007.

FEAR OF CRITICISM

The Issues

Avoiding criticism—that feeling that your weaknesses are exposed for all the world to see—can be as powerful as the fear of embarrassment. No one wants to feel as if they're being judged or talked about negatively, and this can be an issue whether you succeed or fail. Many burgeoning entrepreneurs have been laughed at for ideas others find frivolous, and have then gone on to find tremendous success. Women, especially, can be subject to criticism.

Maxine Clark's Build-A-Bear Workshops (www.buildabear.com) are located around the world. She said that there were many individuals—especially men—who had their doubts about her concept when she first presented it.

"They'd say, 'Why would anybody want to make their own teddy bear? This is only going to last until Christmas,'" Maxine reported having been told. "They didn't get the emotional connection." Until a few years later, that is, when it was clear just how phenomenally successful her venture was turning out to be—recent annual sales reached $360 million.

MILLION-DOLLAR SECRET

"One of the great things about being a woman in business is that most people will think some of these ideas are just silly," shares Maxine Clark. *"The business market has not yet discovered that women are probably the best inventors of all time."*

How to Deal with It

People who take risks and step out of line will always have to endure critics—some they know, others they don't. If you allow yourself to be sidetracked by critics, you are expending your valuable and limited energy in a nonproductive way. In essence, you are giving your critics power and all the minutes, hours, and days you ruminate over their comments only distract you from attaining your goals. This may seem obvious but ceasing or at least minimizing this "rumination" is essential to moving on.

I recall a business situation that upset me greatly. It was not only wasting my time and interfering with my creative thinking, but I also felt emotionally depleted. Unable to get past it, I tried something different: I reached out to a spiritual teacher who was recommended by a friend. He had me do a surprisingly simple exercise. Meditation is not something that I have practiced in my life so the exercise (described below) didn't work for me the first time. The teacher suggested I focus on the person who angered me, with feelings of love. "With love?!" I asked. "How can I feel love when I have such negative feelings?" He said that if you are experiencing anger and are upset, you are choosing to give away control to that person. Once you are able to send the person off with love—real love—without any negative thoughts, then you are truly in control again. This was hard but I eventually realized he was right. I had to do it about five times over a two-week period before finally, I felt free.

EXERCISE

Find a quiet place where you can lie down. Close your eyes and observe the in and out motion of your breath for a few minutes. Imagine and place the person who upset you inside a bubble. Surround the bubble with pink light and send the bubble off with love.

Skepticism and constructive input are invaluable; however, healthy skepticism is often confused with nonproductive cynicism. You'll always find people who are cynical about you and your ideas, no matter what you choose to do. If you believe in your idea, turn a blind eye to them and have confidence in yourself. In fact, take the fear of criticism and make it work for you, like Maria de Lourdes Sobrino of

Lulu's Dessert did. When she launched her ready-made gelatin and dessert company in the United States in the mid-1980s, she said her family didn't expect her to succeed—in fact, they assumed she'd be back to her native Mexico before long. She refused to allow them to say, "I told you so."

"I really took it as a challenge," said Sobrino, "especially to prove to my dad that I was serious about this business. That really kept me going."

For Maria, fear of criticism was the motivating factor that kept her going . . . even during those fleeting moments when she had doubts herself. Today, it is unlikely that anyone would question Maria's success. She has grown Lulu's Dessert into a multi-million dollar enterprise that is ranked among the largest and fastest-growing Hispanic businesses in the United States.

CYNICISM AND SKEPTICISM

Since I frequently speak to women who have internalized cynicism and skepticism about their ambitions, I want to take a moment to clarify this concept. First, let's eliminate any confusion about how the two words are defined.

Cynicism: cynical attitude, beliefs, character, or quality. Synonyms include: pessimism, sarcasm, and suspicion (Encarta Dictionary, 2006).

Skepticism: A [healthy] doubting attitude. An attitude marked by a tendency to doubt what others accept to be true. Synonyms include: uncertainty and doubt (Encarta Dictionary, 2006).

Example: A cynic says, "You can't possibly believe you can really pull this off, can you?" Whereas a skeptic says, "Is it realistic to expect to grow at that rate based on the economic status of the target customers?" See the difference? Skepticism opens constructive dialogue, while cynicism closes possibilities by attempting to end the conversation with intimidation. And remember, cynicism is a reflection of the cynic, not of you or your project.

FEAR OF SUCCESS

Although it may initially seem strange or surprising, fear of success is just as real as fear of failure. That's because with success comes change and the fear of the unknown can be very powerful. A successful business is bound to bring changes in your personal relationships, your social network, and your work life. And for many, change can be frightening even when it's positive.

In my many encounters with women thinking about—or in the beginning stages of—launching their businesses, I've observed a number of common fears. I've also experienced some of these fears myself. Here, we take a look at them, determine how realistic they are, and discuss what to do to take them on.

FEAR OF HARD WORK
The Issues

I have seen and heard two myths about starting and running your own business: that by being your own boss, you'll have more free time, and on the flip side, that you'll never, ever be able to leave work. The reality lies somewhere in between.

In reality, you do have flexibility. For example, you are no longer in the position of having to ask your boss for a day off when your child is sick, when you need to go to the dentist, or if you're planning a long weekend away. However, you'll most likely make up for that time: every woman entrepreneur interviewed for this book said that they work incredibly hard—some, up to 18-hours a day. Many were surprised at how hard they had to work to develop and grow their businesses.

In addition, there are many times when you will choose to spend time at work even when you don't want to. For three years, my husband and I have been apart on his birthday due to an annual tradeshow that he attends for the business. I have missed my daughters' birthdays and even their first day of school. But most days, I am with them for breakfast, take them to preschool, and spend our sacred family time from 4 p.m. to bedtime together. These are tradeoffs that I have found to be acceptable and worthwhile.

"It is very hard work to get there," said Nell Merlino about reaching success. "I'm astounded at how hard it is actually. Yet it's very doable."

How to Deal with It

For most of these women, the rewards of success outweigh the workload. And many of them created their own business to facilitate a better balance between work and family. Although they may be working harder, it's on their own terms (e.g., they can bring their kids to work) and on their own hours (they can take a break from 3 to 5 p.m. every day when the kids come home from school).

Except for some travel demands, this freedom has affected me the same way. For instance, if I want to take my kids to the community pool for an hour during the day, I can make up the work after they go to sleep.

One entrepreneur I know learned the hard way how accustomed he'd become to this flexibility. He decided to sell his business to a larger company and remain on as an employee in exchange for the "security" of a regular paycheck and health benefits. However, when he had to "request" time off for a vacation, he realized he missed his earlier flexibility and freedom and decided to exercise the annulment clause in his sale agreement to become his own boss once again.

Lane Nemeth of Discovery Toys and Petlane also appreciates the advantages of being self-employed.

"I work twice as hard," Lane has said. "But to me, the [trade-off] is the freedom to be creative."

The ability to determine the direction of a business is an enormous privilege. Like Lane, I've experienced the thrill of being my own boss on numerous occasions, by turning my ideas into something real, quickly and with only my say-so. For instance, when I decided to launch the first-ever Mom Invented Store on eBay, I had it up and running within a week. And when I wanted to start a national inventing contest to engage mothers and grandmothers across the country, I pitched the idea to a producer at *Good Morning America* and succeeded (it's since become an annual event on the show).

The upshot is: the fear of hard work is a valid, realistic fear. However, with hard work come rewards. And with entrepreneurship, those rewards are part of your own creation.

FEAR OF GROWTH
The Issues
I'll never forget the excitement and thrill of picking up that first large Purchase Order from the fax machine . . . instantly followed by the horror of trying to figure out how to pay for the production necessary to fulfill it! With the good comes the bad. And there are many challenges inherent with growth, especially rapid growth. It is these challenges—issues like facility expansion, increased personnel, inventory, administration, and legal aspects—that strike fear into the hearts of many new entrepreneurs. They fear they won't have the time, resources, or funds to handle growth.

How to Deal with It
Growth is one of those "good" problems. By facing each challenge you encounter in a measured manner, you will learn to handle even the biggest challenges. And, as you get there you'll find others have had this experience and can assist you.

Teri Gault recalls a major crisis that occurred early on in her business. Her service had garnered an immediate following, with online members who loved what she had to offer. However, one day she woke up to discover that her Web site—the cornerstone of her company—no longer existed. The Web hosting company had gone belly-up with absolutely no warning.

Meanwhile, she had an obligation to meet her members' needs. Fortunately, she had grown a healthy list of customers; the problem was that she suddenly—and without warning—had no way of providing the information they had paid for. Her story ends well—she had backed up every piece of information (a good business practice), including her membership list, which allowed her to e-mail the information to them without missing a week. Although it took a lot of extra time and work, she was able to handle the challenge that growth (and a crisis) had thrown her way.

FEAR OF CHANGING FAMILY AND SOCIAL DYNAMICS
The Issues
Change is inevitable when you launch and grow a business. As you become more invested in the success of your company, your focus and interests change . . . and as a result, your relationships may change as well.

I studied "family systems" in my master's degree program in Marriage and Family Therapy. In essence, when one member of the family changes, it directly impacts the entire family dynamic and the relationships among the family members. By taking the bold step into entrepreneurship, the relationships around the entrepreneur will change.

Julie Clark said her greatest fear when Baby Einstein began taking off was that she wasn't going to have time for her family.

"You always feel torn. It's hard," Julie shared.

And in my family, our children have had to adapt to my erratic work and travel schedule. As I mentioned earlier, one of the hardest parts of being a working mom is that I occasionally have to miss important family events. Although at times it's hard on all of us (sometimes I think it's harder on me than the kids!), I think the positive side is that my girls get to see me working on something I feel passionate about, as well as contributing to the family income. I want my girls to be independent so that they can rely on themselves when they become adults.

Most of the business-moms I interviewed felt the same pull and conflicts that I do, and apply their own creative strategies. For example, Karen Belasco, who founded Good Fortunes cookie company, brought her children to the chocolate factory every day until they were about two or three years old. She feels it's a benefit to her children to see her working.

"They understand the concept that you need to work to earn a living to afford the things that you need in life," said Belasco. "And they see me doing that every day."

How to Deal with It

Take the creative spirit you've tapped into as an entrepreneur to help manage your personal life. Identify what aspects of your life are most dear. Is it being home when your children come home from school? Is it having breakfast with your family? Is it collaborating with your spouse? Use your creativity to work and still maintain your most cherished moments.

With my young kids, I've learned that the "when" is not always the most important factor. When I have a scheduling conflict—for instance, I have to travel on a birthday or special occasion—we come up with solutions and alternatives as a family. We'll celebrate a birthday on a Saturday, when the entire family can be there, rather than Friday, the actual birthday.

And while the pressure of running the business has also taken time away from my extended family, I've tried to counter this by coordinating larger gatherings rather than individual visits to maximize the time I do have. In other words, rather than visit one of my sisters, I'll tell my parents, sisters, and brothers that I'd love to have them all over for a barbecue, or arrange a gathering at the park, the beach, or a restaurant. This way, we can all stay connected and I minimize my time away from work.

Now that her kids are too old to come to work with her each day, Karen Belasco finds more time to spend with them by reminding herself that she is the boss. "I could be the first one here in the morning and the last one here at night," she explained. "But most of the year I'll be out by 2:30 PM so I can pick up the kids from school."

In some cases, the changes can bring families closer together. For example, my sister often watches our children when we need to travel for business. This has made them much closer.

Jeanne Bice of the Quacker Factory, a woman's clothing line sold on QVC, works side-by-side with her son. And Kathy Gendel, founder of Breezies® Intimates—also sold exclusively through QVC—works with her adult daughters to develop new lines.

Still other entrepreneurs feel children respond differently to mom's "job" versus mom's "calling." "[My mother] didn't work because she loved to work. She needed to work," said Julie Clark. "That's different for kids to see than, 'Mommy's doing something she really loves and she's making a difference in the world.' That doesn't mean you have to be an entrepreneur, but if you love your job, I think you are a good role model."

For me, entrepreneurship satisfied one aspect of my Living Dream, which we'll discuss in the next chapter. My husband and I had long aspired to have a business and work together. Between my vision for Mom Inventors, Inc. and my husband's support to help initially fund the business, we built a foundation that allowed him to leave his job and join me full time—thus, fulfilling our dream. Our arrangement also allows us to parent our girls equally. We are all in it together.

RELATING TO OTHER MOMS

The Issues

Several women entrepreneurs who still have young children at home find they are different from the other moms they see every day when dropping off their kids at school.

"I'm a very social person," said Karen Belasco of Good Fortunes. "But when I get to school and I'm interacting with a lot of the other mothers, I feel very different from them."

Despite her success and her confidence as a businessperson, she finds herself at a loss when encountering these moms. She also explains that her core group of girlfriends hasn't changed since childhood and college, because she really hasn't had the time to make a lot of friends outside that group.

I often feel the same sense of discomfort when encountering other moms. For example, I have been asked on occasion to have a play date with my daughter and a child from her class. For the mom inviting me, it is a generous offer and a way to connect. But for me, this simple invitation creates an immediate conflict and at times, feelings of guilt. Play dates always seem to be scheduled during work hours and I have to weigh everything out whether it's an invitation to speak at a women's conference or a chance to go to the park on a play date.

This is where being a mom entrepreneur gets complicated. There is the risk of being judged as rude, but in fact every obligation requires serious consideration—what will I have to give up in order to participate? Nonentrepreneurs may have limited empathy for these conflicts since they may not easily relate the entrepreneurial experience to their own daily lives.

Many of the women featured in this book talked about how hard it is to relate to stay-at-home moms and at the same time how lonely or isolating it can be to be a mom entrepreneur. They talk about how, at times, they actually yearn to simply "hang out" with the kids and family, or just meet a pal or another mom for coffee.

"I have no women friends," said Lane Nemeth. "Sometimes it's very lonely."

Karen Belasco concurs. "I have not built a lot of social relationships with other people that I might have enjoyed in my life."

And the friends you do have may resent the time the business takes away from them.

Every mother, whether she works or not, whether she is an entrepreneur or not, defines what kind of mother she will be. Each of us has had to find comfort in our decisions surrounding the amount of time we spend with our children. Entrepreneurial mothers often believe that their example of working with passion or power has benefits for their children that outweigh the rescheduled parties or missed play dates. I will not argue, or accept, that one direction is superior to another. What matters most is defining motherhood in a way that makes sense to you.

How to Deal with It

With anything in life, there are trade-offs. It is important to prioritize your life and do what you can for those around you. Friendships, like everything else, need to be nurtured, and running a business and taking care of her family is often all a mom entrepreneur can manage. Often the friendships you create end up being with coworkers, colleagues, or business associates. Many of the women I interviewed explained how becoming an entrepreneur weeded out their true friends from their "fair-weather" ones.

"My true girlfriends are proud to be my friend and also very happy with my success," says Madelyn Alfano. "I think they know that I worked really hard for it. A true girlfriend is one who really loves you whether you're rich or poor, tired or not."

Although she hasn't had much time to create new friendships, Karen Belasco takes comfort in the fact that she has a core group of people who she loves and treasures, including old friends, her immediate family, and her extended family.

FEAR OF LOSING YOURSELF

The Issues

As you know, women are givers and tend to nurture their children, husbands, family, and friends, but there comes a time when we need to nourish ourselves. Initially, taking time for oneself feels like a detriment to others and it may be . . . but just for the very short term. The long-term effects of self-nurturing benefit everyone. Of course, being an entrepreneur also puts limitations on one's personal time, but many of the women I interviewed told me that it's essential to find at least some time for yourself.

Teri Gault says the day her Web site unexpectedly disappeared was the day her blood pressure shot up—and stayed there. Since then, she's learned the importance of taking time for herself.

"I tend to make more mistakes when I'm exhausted, because I might make a quicker decision when I'm tired," Teri explained. "When I break down, I'm not a good wife or mother and the company suffers."

How to Deal with It

Teri learned that taking care of herself is something she absolutely has to take time to do. She has a personal trainer come twice a week to her home, so that she can't cancel or fail to show up at the gym. And her colleagues know that she's not available from 9 to 11 every Tuesday and Thursday.

Mary Micucci, who founded Along Came Mary Productions (www.alongcamemary.com), a company that specializes in creating groundbreaking Hollywood and corporate events, also finds it's important to alleviate personal stress with time for herself.

"You have to allow yourself the downtime," Mary explains. "It's hard when it's your own business. But you have to, otherwise you're going to burn out."

EXERCISE

Other methods of taking time for yourself—mark your calendar!

- **Look Inward Regularly.** Find a spot where you can hide out from kids, phones, e-mail, and staff for 10 minutes a day without interruption. Close your eyes and breathe. Sometimes I feel rejuvenated from just taking this short amount of time. In other instances, this short "time out" will provide a moment of clarity.

- **Acknowledge your achievements.** While it's easy to appreciate and relish your children's accomplishments, women tend to overlook their own or brush them aside. Think for a moment about a compliment someone may have given you . . . "You're always on time," or "You're so organized," or "You always say things so well." Let those accomplishments sink in. Women typically trivialize their personal assets. Instead, pause and take note and acknowledge your worthy or even fabulous traits. It's important to remember the reasons you are starting or growing a business: the rewards of entrepreneurship, and your ability to contribute to your family and to the community on a larger scale.

Here's an exercise that can help you honor your achievements:

15-Minute Mental Boost

If this is your first time with this exercise, sit in a quiet space and recall the first day you decided to move forward with your business. If you are just now making that decision, note it.

Write down the first thing you considered an "achievement" (meeting with an advisor, getting incorporated, setting up a Web site, filing a patent, signing a lease, etc.).

Now, list every achievement you recall since then. Once you do that, reread them and underline those of greatest magnitude at the time.

Date ___/___/_____

1 _____

2 _____

3 _____

4 _____

5 _____

6 _____

7 _____

8 _____

9 _____

10 _____

Remind yourself: I am building this business because . . . :

_____

_____

_____

_____

It is important to take stock of what you have accomplished. Revisit this exercise as often as you like but not less than every few months, and especially when you're feeling self-critical or stuck. Then, share your findings with a spouse, loved one, or friend. Often we are so hard on ourselves. When you start looking back at these lists and comparing them with newer ones, you will be amazed with what you actually *do* get done and how you have grown! Tasks that at one point may have seemed to be insurmountable will now seem simple from your expanded vantage point.

FEAR OF CHANGING WORK DYNAMICS
The Issues

Finding success as an entrepreneur can mean your workday role changes and evolves. The fear of changing work dynamics is a valid fear. Some people, for instance, may start a business because they love to cook, only to find that success means they have less time to cook because they need more time to manage personnel, raise capital, or create marketing programs.

One woman I adore used to work with me directly as my publicist. We each loved our regular interaction. However, as her business has grown, she has had to insert others between us. She now spends the bulk of her time managing others and marketing the firm.

I initially started Mom Inventors, Inc. out of the pleasure I get from developing products and building communities. However, as the business has grown, I've been forced to place more time and focus on the financials and raising capital (not my areas of passion or interest). My fear is that I won't be able to perform the tasks that attracted me to my business in the first place.

How to Deal with It

You need to constantly reevaluate your goals and remember that you are the boss. You can prioritize and/or hire smart people to perform many of the tasks you don't like.

MOVING PAST THE FEAR

To overcome the different fears associated with starting your own business, you must make a critical decision: are you going to go for it or not? If you're unsure, the opposite question might help clarify your intention: "What if I *don't* make a change in my life?"

Once you've made your decision, take action and believe in yourself.

MILLION-DOLLAR SECRET

A secret I have heard repeatedly in the interviews is to "speak with intention." For instance, when speaking to Lillian Vernon about my efforts to raise investment capital to fund our growth, she was wise in pointing out my verbal shortcoming: "When you raise capital," not "if," she told me to say. How right she was!

The choice is yours.

Another way to overcome fear? Create a solid plan. In the next chapter, I explain how pinpointing and verbalizing your dreams can translate into a concrete plan of action.

What's *Your* Living Dream? Make It Come True

Starting your own business means changing your life—this is precisely why so many people view entrepreneurship as an opportunity to create something that provides meaning and greater satisfaction in their lives. Sweeping changes start with a vision that includes where, exactly, you want to go, and a plan for how you'll get there.

Because of my own initial discomfort with the idea of creating a business plan—I would rather have visited the dentist—I was reluctant to bring it up this early in the book, in case others share my discomfort. Instead, though, I've tackled it head-on in a way that I hope will be fun. First, I ask you to use your imagination in designing your life dream. Then, I provide exercises that will help you clarify and articulate your personal dreams and ambitions and convert them into a plan of action. The end result will be your first business plan. Or, if you have already created a business plan, you can use this chapter to gauge whether your current direction is in synchronicity with your goals and dreams. (All written exercises that follow in this chapter can be downloaded at www.mominventors.com/millionairemoms.)

When building a business, or any new thing worth creating, "from scratch," it's helpful to have tools to guide you from one point to another. The most fundamental "tool" that you can't do without is belief in yourself, your idea, and the possibility of success. Almost every Millionaire Mom in this book is a firm believer in the importance of passion and belief in herself as the key to her achievements.

In the beginning, critics are your worst enemy. These may include those most near and dear (your parents, your husband, your "well-meaning" friends)—but most particularly your own internal critic: that persistent yammering little voice that reminds you of all the reasons you can't do something and never produces anything positive.

MILLION-DOLLAR SECRET

"The world is out to tell you why you're going to fail. Whether it's your parents, your friends, your husband, the capital (or lack thereof), your manufacturer—I believe you need, in a budding business, these odd kind of blinders that allow you to think, 'they're wrong, I'm right, and I can't fail,'" said Lane Nemeth, who grew Discovery Toys to over $100 million. "That's what I did."

Then there are those niggling fears.

"Fear is the little monkey that sits on your shoulder 24/7 that says, 'You're not educated in this, you can't deliver,'" says Lane. "You've just got to flick it off your shoulder. It doesn't mean it won't come back 20 minutes later, but each time it comes back, just flick it off."

Jeanne Bice took a bit longer to come to this realization. The founder of The Quacker Factory, a $50 million+ company that designs and sells clothing exclusively through QVC, spent a lot of time doubting her own creativity and her own promise as a businesswoman.

"Not believing in myself was one of my biggest mistakes," Jeanne said.

When her husband died suddenly, she owned one struggling retail shop. The harsh reality of her circumstance yielded no other choice but to believe in herself, and at that moment she began conceiving the business that eventually brought her so much success.

YOU ARE YOUR FIRST INVESTOR

Successful businesswomen across the board will tell you that it's critically important to recognize that you are your company's first investor—from the very moment you conceive a business idea. And because you'll need to convince others of your credibility, you need to be able to believe in yourself first.

What does this mean from a practical standpoint? I'll give you a personal example. When I first came up with my invention, the TP Saver™ (a device that prevents kids from unrolling the toilet paper), I struggled to convince myself that this was a viable product and not a hare-brained idea! I asked myself why others hadn't already invented it and whether it was really useful or needed. I searched for similar products on the Internet and in stores. I talked to other parents. I called machine shops and engineers. I learned about plastic manufacturing and the molding process to figure out how the heck to make this thing—all to figure out if people would buy it and how much it might cost to produce. In the meantime, I was also trying to convince *myself* that this idea was a good one.

Once I began to see the possibilities, I told my husband about the idea. He showed moderate interest until I came home from the machine shop one day with a working prototype in hand. He said, "Wow, you are really serious about this." I then took another step. Our local Chamber of Commerce sponsored a workshop on how to write a business plan. Both these steps built credibility with my husband. He knew that if I attended a workshop like this that I was indeed serious, and he became and still is my biggest supporter—something that can't be underestimated when building a business. His support not only reinforced my own belief in myself but also gave me a boost of energy to continue to forge ahead into the unknown.

A WORD ABOUT THE SPOUSE

Many women have told me about their husbands' lukewarm responses to their initial business ideas. As disappointing as this is, taken in context, this is not an unreasonable reaction. If he's focused on his career and other interests, your husband may not consider your idea, at the very beginning stages, to be any more serious than, say, the thought that your child would benefit from Spanish or piano lessons. Once many of these women took action, however—fleshing out their ideas and moving through the first phase—many have been astonished at the support and passion with which their husbands have embraced the business and become actively involved.

If you do not find support from your spouse, you have choices. You can either become bitter and angry, and do it alone, or you can find a group of supportive people who believe in you and your idea.

Victoria Knight-McDowell, the school teacher who founded Airborne Health—a natural health supplement that combats germs—in 1997 and grew it to a $145 million company, also knows the importance of believing in yourself. One of her strategies has always been to "act as if." She had this phrase written in large letters on a big board in the office for everyone to see. "Act as if it's going to happen. Just keep plodding forward. Act as if it's going to happen and just take that next step," Victoria explains.

Debi Davis, founder of FitAmerica MD, shared her thoughts, "Sometimes, when things look the grimmest is when the strength and determination that lives deep inside each and every one of us has an opportunity to emerge," Debi says. "God gives us many gifts. We simply need to have the faith and belief in our ability to succeed."

Before she became a publicist with clients such as Eddie Murphy, Miles Davis, and Janet Jackson, Terrie Williams was a social worker in a difficult financial situation. "I decided I wanted to make money in this lifetime legally and I didn't think it was going to happen in social work. I needed to make a change, and I just saw this article one day, like one paragraph, about a public relations course being taught. Why did I take that course? Because that is what I was called to do."

Once you believe in yourself and the viability of your idea, it's time to convince others. This is when it's important to ask yourself, "What will it take to demonstrate my credibility?" At this stage, it's important to understand that you, the entrepreneur, are the one with the idea, the passion, the energy, and the goals—and that only you can turn your idea into a successful business. And that means creating a plan.

And many of our Millionaire Moms agree. Karen Belasco, whose Good Fortunes cookie company has grown into a multi-million dollar business in just 10 years, succeeded despite not having a solid plan, but says it would have been a lot easier if she'd established one from the start.

"There are certain things I should have done from the get-go. Having an infrastructure in place would have been very helpful," Karen said. "Instead, I winged it and read a few books on how to be an entrepreneur which didn't talk to what I was doing. I think being organized and having a specific plan and some targets to strive for would have been helpful."

Other Millionaire Moms say they could have been successful years sooner if they had had the tools available today that make business planning so much more accessible.

"I probably wasted about 10 years," said Maria Sobrino, Founder of Lulu's Dessert. "I didn't have books at that time. I didn't see or talk to other entrepreneurs. Between understanding the culture, the industry, where to find my supplies, and more—I really lost a lot of time. Today, if you want to build a business, there are so many free seminars, programs, and access to information through the Internet."

And for many, fear sets in when we don't have information, knowledge, and a step-by-step plan. That's why in the next section, I have created a series of exercises that are meant to help you articulate your intention, understand your goals, and unleash your creativity and passion to begin creating that all-important plan that supports your dream.

These exercises are organized into four parts, with an approach that's different from what you might find in most business books. That's because I believe that for most women success begins by establishing an emotional framework and trust in yourself, before you dive into the details of your business. These sections include:

- Formulating Your Fantasy
- Reality-Based Inspiration
- Creating a "Living" Dream
- Taking the Leap

To build your credibility—to yourself and to others—it's essential to move through each of these sections first. The outcome of these exercises will be credibility. The credibility needed to create a solid foundation on which to build your business. Completing these important exercises is part of investing in yourself, and redesigning your future.

"If you have a dream and a burning desire, you can accomplish anything," says Jeanne Bice. "Money will come to you, a business plan will come to you, success will come to you but without desire, it will always be a struggle. You've got to have that passion."

For 16 years, Jeanne had the perseverance and passion to continue growing her business, and then it really took off on QVC in the mid-1990. Read more about her story in her profile later in this chapter.

FORMULATING YOUR FANTASY

What is your deepest dream for yourself—the one you almost don't dare to think about? Are you ready for a change in your life? Whether you're questioning what to do to make that change, or you're already passionate about the product or service you offer, formulating your fantasy can help clarify where you stand right now!

Knowing and truly understanding what you want is critical to changing your life, not in the future, but right now. You must think about it very deliberately. Give yourself the task of identifying your own life fantasy—something that's within your power to create even if it seems like a stretch! Believe me; if it isn't written down, it is not likely to happen. Just writing it down breathes power into the idea.

Specifically, how should you do this? This exercise is twofold:

First, ask yourself, "What is my life's fantasy? What is my big-picture wish?" Maybe it's to be rid of financial fear, to have financial independence, to set your own hours, to give money to your family, to travel, or as is often the case with entrepreneurs, to start something that has not been created before. Whatever it may be, write it down and say it out loud. Writing it is important, but speaking it with intention (i.e., "I intend to . . . ") is the only way to breathe power and life into your fantasy.

As women, our tendency is to give to others, leaving our own needs until the very end, if at all. This time should not be seen as selfish—rather, you are allowing yourself a few moments to dream and articulate what you want. If you are able to create something meaningful to *you*, the result of this has the potential to benefit the lives of those you care about the most.

What is my life's fantasy? _____

_____

My big-picture wish for myself (without consideration of anyone else) is

_____

_____

_____

_____

_____

_____

_____

_____

_____

_____

_____

_____

_____

_____

_____

_____

_____

_____

Now, imagine yourself in your favorite seat in the movie theater watching a film of your fantasy life. You are the star and the film begins at your *current age* and in your *current status*. Allow yourself to let go of any negative "beliefs" you have about yourself (i.e., all the reasons why you can't succeed). Remember that you are not only the star, but also the director, which means you can edit this film completely. If you hear negative talk entering your mind, write it down, under the heading "Beliefs, Untruths, or Things I'd Like to Change" and deal with it later!

While it's important to write it down, be aware that the negative chatter can change its form and sneak in very subtly. Don't be lured in. This is the saboteur of our own inspiration. A wise person once said to me, "When you want to change a pattern, observe it in all its manifestations." So, become almost obsessive in pinpointing it and say, "there it goes again" every time it turns up. Ideally you will write it down each time. By answering these questions, you are, in essence, shaping your vision of yourself. At this point, you are your own skeptic (or cynic). Once you've invested enough effort to have a clear vision of what the fantasy looks like, your own internal investor will be convinced that you are credible enough to move from formulated fantasy to inspired reality.

"My working hard didn't bring me success," said Jeanne Bice. "What brought the success was when I stopped working on it and started believing that I could be a success."

Name of Your Movie	
What are you doing in the film?	
What surprises you about yourself?	
What aspects do you like?	
What aspects do you dislike?	
What would you change?	
Beliefs, Untruths, or Things I'd like to Change. Write down any NEGATIVE TALK about yourself.	

Jeanne Bice

For Jeanne Bice, her success is indisputably linked to passion for her work, belief in herself, and the power of positive thinking. And it shows in her attitude: she is full of high and upbeat energy, along with a great sense of humor, which is part of the secret to why people love her and embrace her products with such zeal.

Jeanne was born in the small town of Fond du Lac, Wisconsin, and went to college at the University of Wisconsin-Milwaukee. While there, she jokes, she vigorously pursued her "MRS." (a title for married women) degree. She succeeded, marrying Arlow Bice, and subsequently became a housewife and had two children, a boy and a girl.

As her children grew older and began to take care of themselves, Jeanne found she had more time on her hands. So, she went into business with a friend and opened a retail store called The Silent Woman, which specialized in gifts and women's clothing. It soon developed a following large enough to open another store in Boca Raton, Florida, although she says it was never very profitable. But not long afterward, in the late 1970s, Jeanne's husband died suddenly, and she was forced to make a living for the first time in her life. The foundation was there—she had begun to design and manufacture her own successful line of clothing—but she had to figure out how to make money.

With the help of her son, she slowly expanded the business. During the early 1990s Jeanne started a label called The Quacker Factory, and began to take notice of a new phenomenon known as home shopping. She became very excited about a network called QVC.

She felt that this would be the perfect forum for her whimsical and entertaining line of clothing—and being the daughter of an auctioneer, she knew she would make a great guest. She eventually got in the door during a national QVC product search, and finally got word she'd been selected to appear. In February 1995, Jeanne Bice and The Quacker Factory made their debut. Her product was the final one on the 3-hour show, and it sold out from previews before it even got on the air. The rest, as they say, is history. Today her annual business tops $50 million. She gives back at least 10 percent of her income each year to charities that range from breast cancer to school scholarships to water treatment plants in Guatemala.

Jeanne is also the author of *Jeanne Bice's Quacker Factory Christmas: Simple Recipes, Fabulous Parties & Decorations to Put Sparkle, Not Stress into Your Season*, as well as *Pull Yourself Up by Your Bra Straps: And Other Quacker Wisdom* (www.quackerfactory.com).

© Photo credit: Gary Kufner

REALITY-BASED INSPIRATION

So you've formulated your fantasy. You can truly envision your life's dream. The next step is taking that fantasy and making a conscious decision to turn it into something actionable.

But first comes inspiration—that intangible element that enables us to believe that our formulated fantasy can actually become something real, and the element that will enable us to move from the theater seat and into production! Oprah calls it the "aha" moment, others call it their turning point—but no matter what it's called, the importance of inspiration cannot be overstated.

How does one get inspired? Jeanne's inspiration came from necessity. You may already be inspired by a person, a product, or an idea—that thing that gets you completely jazzed and ready to change the world. Or, you may need to do work to find that inspiration. Once you find it, you must once again dispel the negative thoughts that inevitably creep in. They have no place during your inspiration moments! Or, for that matter, at any time.

George Bernard Shaw said,

> *"Forget about likes and dislikes.*
> *They are of no consequence.*
> *Just do what must be done.*
> *This may not be happiness,*
> *But it is greatness."*

HOW TO FIND YOUR INSPIRATION

First, identify your sources of inspiration: Look to people with whom you can identify—local figures, other women, those in the same field or with a similar background. Also, people from community groups, television, magazines, news stories, or books.

Next, compare your fantasy with their reality.

Finally, question any reasons their story cannot also be yours. Also, avoid the typical excuses that prevent progress by challenging yourself to defeat each of the following obstacles:

- "I don't have enough money." Few do! When Teri Gault of The Grocery Game (www.thegrocerygame.com) started out, she and her husband were living paycheck to paycheck. So she signed up with a program that offered a free computer if she would sign a long-term contract with an Internet Service Provider (ISP).

  "I was desperate. I was in terrible financial times; I was already doing three jobs . . . the idea of starting a new business was not something that I wanted to do. But I knew I needed to do something, because I was in a trap that I'd never get out of," Teri said. "The Web site was $39 a month and the Internet service was $20 a month. It was $59 a month, but it might as well have been a hundred thousand a month, because I didn't have it." But she believed so strongly in her idea that she persisted . . . and the Grocery Game is now a multi-million dollar business. Talk about creating something out of nothing!

- "I don't have the time." Time is created, not given! Teri had about as much time as she did money, working three jobs to help support her family. But, she said, she knew it was a choice of either doing that forever, or sacrificing the spare moments to change her situation.

- "I don't have the support." You can find the support if you look! Just as Madelyn Alfano opened her second restaurant, she discovered her firstborn infant son, Max, had a life-long mental disability. "I thought, 'Oh God, I've got two restaurants, absolutely no emotional support from Max's father, what am I going to do?' I felt almost helpless," Madelyn explains. But she reversed her thinking and discovered that the support was there. She found the programs and help she needed. Plus, she says, every day her family and friends would come over and work with Max.

- "I don't have the skill." You have a brain, you can learn! Rachel Ashwell didn't have a traditional education or even much experience when she launched Shabby Chic. "I left school at 16, and when I started this company, I didn't really understand any of it," Rachel said. "Life was my lesson. At some point, you have to learn."

Now write down each of the solutions you have created to address each of the obstacles that influence you.

Based on what you have seen others do—and by dismissing all the reasons you "can't"—your "Internal Investor" should now believe that you can change your fantasy into reality, too!

CREATING YOUR LIVING DREAM

Your fantasy + your inspiration is your Living Dream. To tackle this next exercise and create your Living Dream, you must take your deeply held wish and turn it into a "living" project. This living project is your life!

Why is creating a living project so important? Because time goes by quickly, and there's no sense in wasting it—especially if you can envision your fantasy. My mother recently told me how strange it is to age. She's 75 years old, and is living with Parkinson's disease.

"The oddest part of this life is that I still feel 35 years old inside," she told me. "My mind is wildly ready to take on the world and my body is not cooperating."

Hearing her words, I felt a sense of urgency. I realized that my first 40 years have passed in a blink . . . and in 35 years I'll be my mother's age. If this is all the time I have, what do I want to create? This is the foundation of my living dream.

To skip from inspiration straight to creating your business isn't impossible or uncommon, but developing your living dream first will provide both the structure and the support to improve your chances of success and reduce your risk.

"I think the saddest part about women is that we're not geared for business so we don't know how to think 'success.' Someone like Donald Trump thinks success," said Jeanne Bice. "We think, 'Oh, I've got to get the kids to the soccer game, get the laundry done, get to the grocery store, pay the bills, and get dinner ready tonight. And so consequently, we just hang on by the tips of our fingernails. We just hang on. We don't think, 'I could be a multi-millionaire.' But I believe you have to *think* it to *have* it."

WORDS LEAD TO ACTION

It's common to think we'll be "jinxed" or fear the disappointment of falling short of our expectations if we dare to dream or vocalize our goals. But we need to believe in ourselves and communicate our life goals if we ever expect to get what we want out of life.

One of my fondest memories was a tradition that my mom created when I was growing up. At the time I thought everyone did this, but I quickly learned that most families did not. On each of every family member's birthdays, my mother would light the birthday candles and say, "Now, everyone close your eyes and take a quiet moment to think about what wish you would like to have come true." Silence would enter the room as we all bowed our heads and thought deeply. After about two to three minutes, she would say, "Ok, who would like to start?" She established early on that these shouldn't be pie-in-the-sky or unattainable dreams like, "I want to save the world," but instead more realistic wishes like, "I want to do well on my math test," or "I would like to spend more time with the family," or "I'd like to sell brownies on the street."

The purpose of this candle-lighting tradition was to "speak with intention" about what we wanted. My mother also firmly believed that if we expressed our inner thoughts and dreams out loud, then the family could help in attaining them. Now that we're adults who continue this tradition, it is amazing how we continue to work to help the others get what they wish for—whether it's by making business introductions, offering financial support, or giving emotional support.

"LIVING DREAM" EXERCISE

Today is your birthday. I am lighting a candle for you. Now, close your eyes and make a wish. Even if you are by yourself right now, say the wish out loud. Say it out loud with conviction! Shout it if you have to! Say, "My intention is to make [blank] happen." This will help you begin creating your living dream. This living dream is how you'll transform your fantasy into reality. With your living dream, you are stating your bold intention—a necessary step that will help you internalize your decision, believe it yourself, and turn that fantasy into something tangible.

Writing it down is critical. Don't edit as you write. Allow yourself the freedom to write and don't give your internal critic any
airtime. If you hear the critic, shout "STOP!" if you have to. This
technique may seem ridiculous; however, it is part of re-training
your mind to do away with the internal critic. In psychological
terms, this is called "Cognitive Restructuring. This is your time to
be free to explore without anyone criticizing the process (including you).

My "Living Dream" is to

_____

_____

_____

_____

_____

_____

_____

_____

_____

_____

_____

_____

_____

_____

_____

_____

_____

_____

_____

COGNITIVE RESTRUCTURING

People are often unaware of the negative voice that lives covertly in our unconscious mind. I have touched on this "chatter" earlier in our movie theater exercise. But it's so important that I want to discuss it a bit further.

In the early 1960s, Aaron T. Beck, MD, was working with depressed patients. In the course of his work he found a commonality—that most of them experienced "streams of negative thoughts that seemed to pop up spontaneously." He termed these cognitions "automatic thoughts," and discovered that their content fell into three categories: negative ideas about themselves, the world, and the future.

Dr. Beck theorized that how we think (cognition), how we feel (emotion), and how we act (behavior) all interact together. Specifically, that our *thoughts* determine our feelings and our behavior. (To learn more go to www.beckinstitute.org.)

However, we don't need to be depressed to experience these automatic thoughts. In fact, I believe most of us have heard these negative thoughts at different times in our lives, especially when we are considering taking risks or hoping to redirect the course of our lives.

So why is this important? Our personal lives intimately drive our business lives. And according to the Center for Mind-Body-Medicine, a division of American Health Research Institute, "Self-defeating thoughts, negative self-talk, and irrational beliefs are the cause of much of the stress in our lives. Most people are not aware of their stress-producing thinking."

And that, of course, can lead to failure before you even start! Fortunately, there's a technique to help correct this negative thinking called "Cognitive Restructuring." It is intended to help you deliberately alter your thought patterns.

When you start to think those distressing thoughts—and they can come hard and fast. With conviction, say out loud: "Stop!" Then say, "I don't have any more energy for this kind of thinking."

By recognizing and identifying the thoughts right when they're happening, you too can help dispel negative thinking. Take comfort in knowing that you are not alone!

Even the most successful women—like Lane Nemeth—recognize the "monkeys" that can cause negative thoughts. Like Lane, learn to "flick them off your shoulder" right when they come!

TAKING ACTION

Would you ever dare attempt to drive from California to New York by randomly getting in your car and driving east—without a road map? I don't even drive two blocks in Los Angeles without www.mapquest.com. Really! The same is true for your business. If you plan to create a business (especially a highly successful one) it's important to consult an overall map so that you know where you are going.

Unfortunately, you can't go to your local AAA and pick up a pre-marked TripTik®. However, I will outline here the steps you need to create one yourself —built for your own specific journey. It's not difficult—all it takes is some thought and some soul-searching. And once you follow these steps, you'll have the road map that will help lead the way toward your living dream.

The first step—if you are at the very early stages, and you know you'd like to do something different, but you're just not sure of the direction in which you should be going—is to ask yourself, "What do I know?" Then ask, "What am I passionate about?" Now write it down.

THE INSIDE STORY

Lane Nemeth

Lane Nemeth has built her vision into a highly successful business—not once, but twice! In 1978 she found herself frustrated by her inability to find just the right products for her baby daughter Tara, so she took it upon herself to solve the problem. The direct sales company she founded, Discovery Toys, which sold educational toys, books, and games through representatives who'd host home parties, eventually grew into a $100 million business, which she sold to Avon in 1997.

Today Lane has used the knowledge she gained from Discovery Toys to launch a new business. This one was inspired when her daughter, now grown, brought home her first "grand dog," a Cavalier King Charles Spaniel named Jade. Again, she tried to buy the best products and food for Jade, but found it a challenge. So after months of research and scouting out high-quality products, she founded Petlane (www.petlane.com). She chose the direct sales model once again due to its personal approach and its ability to enable individuals—her "Pet Advisors"—to satisfy their entrepreneurial spirit with minimal investment and lots of support and training. It also allows them to explain the value of the products to potential consumers in a personal, intimate setting.

When asked what it takes to nurture an idea, Lane replied, "I think it takes a vision. You need to know where it's going right from the budding stage. You can't sort of just sit there and say 'I have this tiny little seed, and I have no idea what the plant's going to look like.' You must know what the plant's going to look like, in both those stages. [For me,] I knew it looked like parties, and I knew it looked like helping parents, and I knew it looked like helping people choose dreams. So I had a vision."

© Photo credit: Bill Newell

For example, when Rachel Ashwell was in the midst of a divorce, with a newborn and a two-year-old, she was forced to think about her next steps with immediacy. So she sat down at the kitchen table and asked herself, "What do I know?" Growing up, both her parents were experts in the antique industry. As a child she had accompanied her father to flea markets to scout out and purchase antique books. Her mother specialized in restoring old dolls. This was something that surrounded Rachel as a child, and talents she had nurtured herself in her personal life. So she turned her skills to purchasing old furniture and restoring it, opening her first store with limited inventory and a shoestring budget. It was the beginning of Shabby Chic, and success grew from there.

Once you've pinpointed your strengths and your passion, you've created the means by which you will reach your "Living Dream." Now it's time to create a clear road map to get you there. Doing so will create clarity that will reduce fear, ward off the critics, and build your confidence to move forward. Even if you have already launched your business, it can be helpful to take the time to re-think your approach.

Now that you've clarified and announced your intention, which is the foundation of your Living Dream, this next section will help you put your Living Dream into action.

CREATING YOUR OWN PERSONALIZED ROAD MAP
Here's an exercise to help you create your road map or to find a new and better route:

- **Clarify your vision.** Ask yourself what you are building. Is it a service or product you'd like to offer? The answers to this question will help create a structure for achieving your Living Dream. (For example, if your living dream is to build a life-changing business that combines your love of gardening and creative solutions, it may look something like this: "Build a successful gardening company that specializes in providing competitively priced garden tools specifically designed and decorated for women gardeners.")
My vision is to

_____

_____

_____

_____

_____

- **Develop your mission.** Why does this product or business exist? What does it aim to accomplish? When you have answered these questions, you have stated your mission. If you follow the gardening tool example, the mission might be, "Fulfill the growing demand from women in the gardening market by developing the most attractive, gender-specific tools available at a broadly affordable price-point."
My mission is to

_____

_____

_____

_____

_____

- **State your goals.** What are your specific short- and long-term goals? Note, your long-term goals should also relate to the outcomes of your "Living Dream." Once you write them down, you will have a list of objectives that you can later measure. (For

example: By August 2008, I will sell 5,000 units of my gardening tools to hardware stores in my area. In my second year, I
will sell 25,000 units to 100 stores nationwide.)

My short- and long-term goals are to (be specific!)

_____

_____

_____

_____

_____

- **Set your strategies.** What measures will you employ to build
your company over time? Be specific! These will become your
strategies. (For example: I am initially going to sell my product
to small independent stores and then move into bigger chain
stores by leveraging the sales in the smaller stores. I will then
expand into other markets, such as Wal-Mart and drug and grocery chain stores that offer garden centers to their customers.
For now, don't worry if you can't get too specific. Your marketing plan, related to this section, will undoubtedly be further
refined as you read the next chapter.)

My strategies are to

_____

_____

_____

_____

_____

- **Create a plan.** What is the work to be done? Create an action
plan with specific tasks to be accomplished on specific due
dates. If you miss a due date, don't feel like a failure, just assign
a new date. Suggestion: tackle the "easy" tasks first and try to
check off one task per day. But even for the "dreaded" ones,
usually the anticipation of the task and the story you've created
around doing the task (story: the store owner will say "no") is

worse than actually doing it. (For example: I recently walked into a local craft store to pitch our Tidy Table Covers™. Sales still aren't one of my favorite tasks, but it needs to be done. The "story" that I told to myself was that the owner would not be interested initially and put me off for months. The outcome of the sales meeting came as a pleasant surprise, however. The retailer loved the product so much that they offered to display it at an upcoming tradeshow where they were exhibiting. I asked the cost. They said, "We love the product and want to see you do well. We won't charge you anything." Wow! That was a surprise. A dreaded task became an exciting business coup thanks to the generosity of the lovely business owner and a wish to pass on good fortune!)

Now, to remind yourself *why* you are going to be doing all these things, rewrite your "Living Dream" here:

I will do these things because my "Living Dream" is to . . .

_____

_____

_____

_____

_____

My plan is to . . . (Answer questions from section above "Create a Plan.")

What is the work to be done . . .

_____

_____

_____

_____

_____

I am grateful to my friend, Jim Horan, for making this process easier for me with his book, *The One Page Business Plan*. For more help creating your road map, visit www.onepagebusinessplan.com—an excellent tool for entrepreneurs. Then, as you begin formulating your business, here are some of the specific steps you'll need to take:

- **Name your company.** What's in a name? A whole lot, especially when you're building relationships and an image with buyers, vendors, and customers. That's why choosing an effective name is a vital early step in developing your business. One of the most common mistakes I see is naming your company too narrowly. For example, if you invented a day-glo dog leash and you name your company "Day-Glo Dog Leashes, Inc." it would be tough to release any other pet product or to offer a pet grooming service under the same company name. When Lane Nemeth, for example, launched her company that sells high-end pet products, she named it www.petlane.com, a carefully selected, broad name that could include virtually any pet product or service as she moves into the future. In, considering a name, you should also determine whether the corresponding Web address is available—particularly if your customers, partners, or vendors are likely to seek you out on the Web. You can determine if the name you would like is available as a Web site address by going to www.register.com or other similar services.

- **Get business cards.** When I worked at the White House, a colleague from the White House Communications Office said to me, "Your proposal isn't real until it's in writing." This statement holds true regarding a business card as well. Once your company name and logo are in print, you've established it as a real entity to the outside world (and to yourself).

- **Create workspace.** I first launched Mom Inventors, Inc. from my second daughter's bedroom. For her first year she slept in a bassinet in our master bedroom so that I could have an office space. Eventually we renovated the garage into a workspace. Whatever you decide to do, I encourage you to create a defined workspace. I found the kitchen table difficult because I was constantly clearing my work for meals and my daughters' art projects. So even if it means a card table and a chair in the corner that's all yours, I suggest you do it!

- **Create a set work schedule.** If you're taking care of the kids, you should harbor no illusions that your children will quietly read books and color while you conduct business. While research, planning, and writing can be accomplished at night or during naptime, it is important to arrange some workday childcare coverage—even if it is only a few hours per week. If paid help isn't feasible, look to family members or community services for help. The key is to arrange the same hours each week that you can use and depend upon to schedule important telephone calls or outside meetings. Then, expand your babysitting coverage when possible. You may not accomplish everything on your list during these fleeting time slots, but you can begin to tackle the most critical items on your list and build momentum.

- **Create a wish list of resources.** Even if you can't afford anything on this list right now, it is important to know what you need. List the concrete things first—computer, fax machine, extra phone line, etc.

  Next, list the support you need. When I started out, I did not have a proper accounting system. I typed up each of our invoices as Word documents. This made it very difficult to keep track of the finances. When I first hired a bookkeeper, she had to spend hours recreating our financials. At first, all I could afford was five hours per week of the bookkeeper's time, and she was worth every penny. Now, nearly three years later she is still with us. Do what you can to set up things properly to save yourself time, money, and frustration.

- **Establish your benchmarks/objectives.** Decide what you want to achieve with your business . . . and by what dates. Be very specific.

SUPPORT IS OUT THERE!

If you aren't receiving the support you feel that you need from family and friends, broaden your framework and reach out to your community. You can define "community" any way you wish. It may mean joining national organizations like NAWBO (National Association of Women Business Owners) or attending meetings provided by your local Chamber of Commerce. Just be sure to keep reaching out until you find the colleagues and mentors who offer you the support you need.

In 1958, my mother suddenly became a single parent of four children under the age of six—with no child support. I grew up wondering how she managed.

"I couldn't have done it without the community of women that surrounded me," she explained to me. "We lifted each other up during the most difficult times."

From this I learned that sometimes you just need to look outside your immediate "comfort zone" to recognize that you are not alone. Why wait? If you need support, seek it out. I have found that support comes in the most unexpected ways, but no one will help you if you don't let them know what you are creating—or if you don't ask! Even better—help someone else. It doesn't take long before gratitude, laughter, and helpful exchanges of information become the fabric of support that will become your community.

TAKE THE LEAP!

Some of the Millionaire Moms in this book were inspired to create a business out of desperation and the need for survival. Others wanted to change the direction of their lives for different reasons—they were tired of the corporate drain, like Tomima Edmark, who invented what became the multi-million dollar TopsyTail business. Regardless of what initially inspired them, all of them, without exception, had to make a decision at some point to just go for it. It's at this point when perceived obstacles can cause even the most inspired entrepreneur to stop in her tracks. For many, even the thought of writing a business plan is often one of those obstacles.

You'll hear again and again that writing a business plan is an essential step. The bad news? I agree with this advice: you've got to do it. The good news? You already have done it! Much of the work has already been done through the exercises in this chapter, and specifically the "Creating Road Map Exercise." You simply need to extract and modify a few words and *voilà!*—you'll have your first business plan!

As you can probably already gather, the purpose of a business plan is to help you translate what you are thinking into something that's actionable. Writing down anything helps you focus on results. Plus, the experience of writing a business plan can help broaden your thinking and give you the tools necessary to clearly articulate your plans to others. It is gratifying to revisit your plan every few months to see what you have accomplished, to see what you still have to accomplish, and to add any variations to the plan based on changes that have occurred.

The task of fully creating your plan can take five minutes, five days, or five weeks, depending on your goals. But no matter what format your business plan takes, remember that it is an evolving document that changes over time as your product, service, or company develops. Once you have a plan, modify and update it as necessary. There are plenty of books and Web sites that will help you on your way (see www.mominventors.com/millionairemoms for these exercise templates and a list of suggested resources).

Although a few of the entrepreneurs interviewed for this book found success despite the lack of a solid plan, most of them say that if they could go back and change something, it would be to plan more effectively. With hindsight, writing a business plan might have meant earlier success and/or fewer mistakes.

For some absurd reason, there is a great deal of embarrassment or shame around not knowing how to design or understand a business plan. Wouldn't it be equally as ridiculous for a person to walk up to a grand piano and expect to know how to play without instruction? Why then should we feel this way? There are tools and resources that are readily available to everyone today—not just those in school or the business world—it's now easier than ever to find the information to create your plan and leap.

MILLION-DOLLAR SECRET

"To be successful you have to be passionate. You have to be smart in your planning. You have to really know who your target market is and how you're going to get your product to market," says Madelyn Alfano, owner of Maria's Italian Kitchens, one of California's largest woman-owned restaurant chains. *"You have to educate yourself and find people to help."*

A PLAN FOR THE FUTURE

Friends and family, angel investors, banks, and venture capitalists will more likely be attracted to your company when they can see that you have done your homework and can *speak* your intention to succeed. When you believe in yourself it comes across both verbally as well as in the way in which you carry yourself. There is no room here for arrogance or illusions. Investors (including yourself) want to hear the truth. If you can articulate your vision, goals, and plans clearly and combine those elements with drive and passion, nothing will prevent you from catapulting your business into the marketplace and succeeding.

In the next chapter, I'll give some concrete advice on how you can do just that by using creativity to structure your business, and by providing strategies for creating awareness and building your brand.

Businesses without Borders: Creative Structuring and Marketing

Most of the Millionaire Moms in this book launched their companies with little or no business experience with backgrounds as diverse as social work, teaching, retail, acting, and stay-at-home mom. Yet they've achieved extraordinary results. In fact, many of them have found remarkable success because they weren't beholden to conventional business thinking. They were free to create, and that's exactly what they did.

In this chapter we'll talk about "businesses without borders"— about how these women applied creative ways to help a business grow and thrive—and how you can, too. Specifically, we'll discuss the importance of positioning and branding your company, interesting and creative ways to structure your business, sales strategies that will connect you with your customer, and how to take advantage of the free media to help get the word out.

While I encourage trying nonconventional approaches to your business, I will familiarize you with some proven tools and methods for building a business.

START AT SQUARE ONE—YOUR MARKETING PLAN

A main component of organizing any business is developing a marketing plan. In that plan you will define your market position, establish a sales structure, and build your "brand." Aside from your company's unique product or service, these factors will set you apart. Now, you may be thinking, "I just did a plan" in Chapter 2. The marketing plan is a strategic component of your business plan. Think of this as refining your Goals, Strategies, and Next Steps—you will think through and document more specifically how you will make money.

In my own experience of developing my business—and through the process of interviewing the other successful businesswomen—I have discovered that a combination of creativity and hard work is crucial to carrying out a successful marketing plan. The following are steps that will help you formulate a strong marketing plan to position your company as unique and create a sales strategy that will bring success.

DEFINE YOUR POSITION

Before you do anything, it's important to define your unique position in the marketplace. This will provide the basis for communicating who you are—and why you are different—to everyone you encounter, including potential buyers, the media, and, ultimately, your customers.

To define your market position, ask yourself questions like these: What is different about my business? What's my marketing angle? What's unique? Is it my community? Is it my price point? Do I have something rare or is it the same thing that is already out there, but with a new twist? Is the difference the way I service the client or the way I deliver the product or service?

Maxine Clark is a prime example of how positioning and branding is essential. She is not the first person to sell teddy bears and stuffed animals. In fact, she entered an incredibly saturated field when she founded her business, Build-A-Bear Workshop, in 1997. What differentiates her company is her position and her brand—Build-A-Bear Workshop isn't just another teddy bear, it's a stuffed animal that children can design and create themselves. In addition, the process of "building" the bear creates a bonding experience between children and their caregivers, and a unique connection between the child and the toy. Her position in the marketplace differentiates the company from all other competitors.

"I didn't invent teddy bears or factories that make them, and I wasn't the first one in the make-your-own-stuffed-animal business," Maxine explained. "But I knew what to do with it, and that's really the biggest problem—a lot of people just don't know what to do with what they have."

"One of the most influential moments in my life is when the then Chairman of The May Company, Stanley Goodman, said, 'Retailing is entertainment and the store is a stage and when the customer has fun, they spend more money,'" continues Maxine. "Hearing such a statement from the CEO at that time set my course and the light bulb went on."

Terrie Williams' core philosophy of honoring humanity fit her approach to launching her business. Prior to starting her public relations company, she had met Eddie Murphy and several of his associates. " . . . Everyone is someone, and if you honor that in everyone, amazing things happen," says Terrie. Through this approach she was able to earn the respect of those around Eddie Murphy—who happened to be the top box office draw in America at that time—and ultimately sign him as her first client.

Debi Davis of FitAmerica MD is another example of how positioning differentiated her in an otherwise saturated marketplace. When she launched her initial weight-loss products in the 1990s, she was very deliberate in how she positioned them.

"I didn't like that diets were rigid. I didn't like that people had to buy a six-month plan or a one-year plan," Debi explained. "I didn't like the inflexibility, so we did the opposite of what a lot of businesses did."

She allowed her customers to purchase what they needed when they needed it—and her meal plans were less rigid and more realistic. The strategy helped Debi build her company into a $45 million operation.

MILLION-DOLLAR SECRET

"Howard Schultz (of Starbucks) didn't invent coffee and Ray Kroc (of McDonald's) didn't invent hamburgers," explains Maxine Clark. "It doesn't mean you have to invent the idea; it's just—how can you make it better?"

Maria Sobrino had a different set of circumstances when she founded her business. Her product was, in fact, completely unique to the marketplace. Pre-made gelatin desserts, in the tradition of her Mexican culture, were not available in the United States when she launched her business in the mid-1970s. She initially positioned her product to bring the taste of Mexico to first-generation Mexicans living in America, who would recognize a taste of "home." She knew there was a sizable immigrant population that would consume a dessert unavailable in the U.S. market. Because her market eventually grew beyond her initial target audience—and large competitors like Jell-O launched competitive products years later—her position as the "first" and original, and as a Mexican-American woman offering an authentic taste of home, has continued to serve her company well. (Her company sold 60 million dessert cups last year.)

Julie Clark had a similar experience. She also brought something wholly unique to the marketplace. One day she set out to purchase educational videos for her children, only to discover that what she was looking for didn't exist. So she borrowed a video camera and created her own, which was the start of Baby Einstein.

TAKE INVENTORY

Once you've defined your unique position in the marketplace, do a little company "soul-searching"—taking inventory of your business's strengths and weaknesses. Having this type of clarity from the outset will help build and strengthen your company's foundation, so you'll end up spending less time later back-tracking or troubleshooting a situation gone wrong.

When I launched Mom Inventors, Inc., for example, I recognized that my strengths included my experience working on national issues as a former presidential appointee in The White House, my ability to make connections with other moms, and my understanding of the media. On the other hand, my weaknesses included a lack of capital, a lack of specific experience in product development, and no sales distribution network to tap into.

Maxine Clark, on the other hand, had lots of retail experience and countless contacts from her former role as a president of a $2.5 billion company. She also had $2 million of her own money to invest—more than most entrepreneurs ever dream of starting with! However, she had a big vision for her company, and she knew she needed more capital, which was a big challenge. She ended up securing an angel investor who believed as strongly in her vision as she did, investing $4.2 million of his own money.

Deann Murphy, founder of Distlefink Designs, was working at a research center at Columbia University which suddenly lost its federal funding, and she lost her job. While one of her strengths was crafting—she was an excellent quilt-maker—she had no experience or education in business when she founded her company.

"I wasn't brought up to run my own business," explains Deann. "I had no business experience. If I had not backfilled it with rational decisions, it would have never taken off." Deann basically taught herself everything as she went along: product development, marketing, sales distribution, and so much more.

Once you've honestly established what you bring to the table—and what you lack—it's time to get resourceful. For most people, money is the first item on their list of challenges—a subject covered in depth in the next chapter. But also consider creative methods that can help you avoid the need for money entirely. How can you use what you already have to address your needs?

TAKING INVENTORY

Whether you're just starting your business or you're years into running it, the following simple exercise can help you evaluate your assets and challenges.

Draw a line down the center of a piece of paper. Ask yourself the following questions and make a list of your answers. On the left side of the line write down your assets: what strengths do you bring to the company—skills, capital, knowledge, contacts, etc.? On the right side write your challenges: what weaknesses do you need to acknowledge and address?

When I conceived of the idea to create an online store, for instance, I didn't have the money or infrastructure in place to hire a techie to set it up. So I researched my options and decided to create an eBay store. eBay already had the infrastructure in place, it was low-cost, and it was fast and easy to set up. We even turned it into a benefit, positioning our presence on eBay in a unique way—as the "First-Ever Mom Invented eBay store." We sent out a press release that generated media coverage and gave the store a sales boost! It's the way your offerings are positioned and presented that can create perceived value among your customers.

Jeanne Bice used to manufacture all The Quacker Factory's apparel in her own factory. Although the company was growing, the stress of running the manufacturing end was taking a toll.

She explained that one day her son (and business partner) sat her down and asked what she thought her strengths were. Managing the manufacturing was not one of them, she said, and they decided to restructure. Today Jeanne still designs and sells the clothes—but outsources their production to numerous vendors. She explains that it allows them to focus on their core competencies—and has significantly reduced their stress levels!

"You learn your strengths and find somebody else to do the other things," explains Jeanne. "You don't have to do it all."

MILLION-DOLLAR SECRET

Jeanne Bice explains the importance of changing direction when necessary:

"Say your best friend makes the best chocolate chip cookies in the world and gives you the recipe—and you make the recipe and your cookies come out badly, you'll make them a second time and a third time but you will not go beyond that . . . you'll find another cookie recipe. In business, women need to follow the same advice—if the recipe fails, don't keep using it over and over again. Get another recipe, lady!"

"You need companies made up of people with different skills, and you have to know what your strengths are," explains Maxine Clark. "You have to depend on a team of people to help with any project, whether it's somebody designing a store, or a lawyer reviewing the trademarks. You learn to use the resources to get things done."

Julie Clark agrees. "Know what your weaknesses are and get somebody else to do those things." She explains how her husband made up for her lack of organizational skills, and how that made a big difference when they went to sell the company and had thorough, well-organized financial books to present. (They sold to Disney for $50 million.)

Think about how you can work with what you already have, and then think about ways in which you can further structure your company to maximize those strengths. Sometimes it's helpful to brainstorm with others. Connect with other businesspeople who you admire, and ask questions about how they do things. Or create an advisory board of professionals who bring unique strengths to the table, such as sales, advertising, accounting, etc. It's never too late—Maria Sobrino only recently created an advisory board in order to help take her company to the next level.

CREATING STRUCTURE THAT WON'T BOX YOU IN

Once you've evaluated your strengths and weaknesses, it may help you think more clearly about how you'd like to structure your business. For instance, if you are an exceptional public speaker, you may consider selling primarily on a home shopping network or infomercial. If you are a whiz at Web programming, an Internet-based business may be for you.

It's interesting to note how the Millionaire Moms structured their companies in very unique ways—many of which had never occurred to me while I was structuring my own. Even if you've already structured your business, there's much to learn from others' successful strategies. You may be able to weave some of them into your own company to see if they work. What I found most relevant from their examples, though, was not the specific methods they used. It was the innovative mindsets with which they approached the challenge of structuring their businesses and the way in which they approached growing their sales that were most provocative to me.

Over the years Teri Gault had spent every Saturday morning clipping coupons, looking up local grocery sales, and matching coupons with rock-bottom sale prices to strategize and stockpile purchases. Her habit had saved her thousands of dollars a year. She established an Internet-based business for her local region to share this information with others, and has since created a business model to expand the company nationally. She's structured it by licensing the use of "Teri's List" by zip code, offering individuals franchise opportunities in their own region—supplying the grocery and coupon information to consumers in their local areas. In other words, a businessperson in your hometown can license the use of Teri's List and create her own home-based business.

Debi Davis also franchised Fit America. Her franchises were actual brick and mortar retail stores, rather than Internet-based businesses. These franchises were enormously successful. However, Debi advises, " . . . do be sure to maintain control if you take the franchising route."

"I lost control of the franchisees because I lost control of their members," Debi explains. They'd photocopy four-color brochures, change meal plans, and make other changes that affected the continuity of the business. In retrospect, she would have maintained a centralized database of all the franchisees' customers. Although she has since remedied the problem, it became a challenge trying to get franchisees to follow her vision.

Lane Nemeth, who launched Discovery Toys in the 1970s, took a different tack, modeling it after the Tupperware structure with a direct sales approach. She recruited sales representatives, "Educators," who would host house parties to sell her educational toys. She wanted these reps to be extensions of herself; people who cared about the products and their effect on children, and who could educate consumers directly about their benefits. Lane believed that the house parties were essential because if consumers could see, feel, and understand the benefits of the toys, they'd be more likely to purchase them. Her model specifically circumvented the typical retail distribution channels, such as large retail store chains. The plan worked! She has since followed a similar model for her new company—Petlane, which offers specialty pet products.

Rachel Ashwell initially started out opening one Shabby Chic retail store in Southern California. It was an overnight success. Since then she's opened nine additional stores, but has expanded her vision well beyond retail, diversifying with books, a TV show, and by licensing a line of home furnishing products to Target stores under the brand name of Simply Shabby Chic®. She also manufactures her own line of furniture and bedding under the Shabby Chic brand. Rachel explained that each of these areas could be its own business; and that the benefit of this expanded approach is that it's kept things interesting *and* diversified. When one area of the business doesn't perform as well, the others fill in the gaps and keep the company humming. By developing different channels for growth, rather than relying on one product in one industry, Rachel has reduced risk and created enormous success.

In 1951, Lillian Vernon first conceived of selling products by mail order. She designed a purse and a belt that could be personalized, placed a $495 ad in *Seventeen* magazine, and promptly received $32,000 in orders—a lot of money in 1951! Today, the company still specializes in personalization, and has expanded to offer household items, gifts, children's products, and fashion accessories—still through direct catalog as well as online sales.

Your company structure can also change over time. Karen Belasco started out selling her Good Fortunes giant fortune cookies strictly wholesale—to retailers like Bloomingdales, FTD, and 1-800-Flowers. A few years ago, however, she decided to add on a consumer-oriented approach, and now offers her products directly to customers via her Web site, www.goodfortunes.com, as well as through wholesale outlets. Although it was a shift in strategy that demanded a capital investment, Karen says it's made a big impact.

Deann Murphy also changed her sales structure over the 25 years she was in business. When she founded her company in 1972, she sold her innovative make-your-own quilt kits through retailers like Bloomingdale's, B. Altman & Co., and Macy's. As the business evolved and she began selling new products, she adopted new distribution channels. For instance, when she launched her Yarn Crafter product, she sold through television marketers—basically, selling by infomercials. Today they're extremely common—and successful—but at the time she was a pioneer. These 60-to-80-second commercials would demonstrate the product and provide an 800 number for customers to order on the spot. Then, later, with products like the BeDazzler, she sold through specialty retail channels again, such as craft and toy stores.

"I owned the business for 25 years, and I've had many stages," said Deann. "And at each stage, I had to learn new things."

What we can learn from these women is that there isn't just one correct way to build a business. It is exciting to recognize that there are many different ways to position and structure our companies. Once you are aware of the different models that are available, then it is important to pick or create strategies that feel right to you and go for it!

THE INSIDE STORY

Maria de Lourdes Sobrino

Maria de Lourdes Sobrino combined creativity and common sense—along with a great work ethic—to structure and build her business, Lulu's Dessert®, into the $10 million business it is today (www.lulusdessert.com).

Born and raised in Mexico City, and the mother of two grown daughters, Maria first created a business in the tourism industry with an initial focus on organizing conventions and events. She later expanded her business to a travel agency, which grew so rapidly that she decided to open an office in Los Angeles. In 1982, Maria had to close her Mexican travel business due to the unstable economic conditions in Mexico; however, her entrepreneurial spirit grew stronger and she began to explore other passions and ideas.

Maria came upon the idea of selling ready-made gelatin products when she couldn't find those desserts in the United States. A staple in her native Mexico, these products were considered a novelty when she introduced them to American grocers. Maria recognized a need, filled it, and revolutionized the food industry by creating the first-ever ready-to-eat gelatin category, based on her own mother's recipe.

From the initial production of 300 cups of gelatin a day, Lulu's Dessert® has overcome many challenges and obstacles to become a leading maker of ready-made desserts. The company recently expanded its facilities to Vernon, California, where it manufactures products currently distributed in domestic and international markets. This year she will produce 60 million cups of 50 different products, including gelatin, flan, rice pudding, parfait, and more.

Maria was invited to lend her expertise to a special commission created by U.S. President Bush and former Mexico President Fox. The commission, "Partnership for Prosperity," will help identify new ways to increase investment in remote parts of Mexico that generate a large percentage of immigration to the United States.

She participates in the following Advisory Boards: the California Hispanic Chamber of Commerce (CHCC); *Latina Style Magazine* in Washington, D.C.; and Nacional Financiera (NAFIN), an investment bank in Mexico. She also serves as an advisor to Rancho Santiago Community College Foundation, and NAWBO Enterprise Institute. In addition, she is a founding member of the Working Families for Wal-Mart steering committee.

In May 2007, she will share her story along with interviews with outstanding Latinas and their success stories in her first book, *Thriving Latina Entrepreneurs in the United States*.

BUILDING YOUR BRAND

Once you decide on a particular business model such as direct sales, retail, Internet, catalog, franchise, or something entirely different, it's important to identify what needs to be done. How will you implement your approach or strategy? How will you take your company's unique position and sell your products or service to the world?

An important place to start is by building your brand. Branding goes beyond positioning to create a connection between your company and your customers. It involves establishing an emotional connection whereby consumers identify with you and your product or service (and that, in turn, makes them want to buy it). Companies like Nike, Pepsi, and Apple wield tremendous influence as a result of their brand-building efforts. But that doesn't mean you have to have a Nike or Apple budget to build your brand.

In his excellent book, *The Little Red Book of Selling*, Jeffrey Gitomer shares great tips on how to build a solid foundation for your company strategically through branding yourself as an individual.

" . . . It's how hard you work, how smart you work, and how dedicated you are, combined with your self-belief, that will help your brand proliferate more than anything," explains Jeffrey.

I think his tips on personal branding are right on the mark:

- "Create demand for your product or service indirectly. (Through means other than direct advertising.)
- Get the business community to have confidence in your business. Earn a reputation for quality performance so good that it's talked about.
- Establish yourself as an expert. Why just be in the field, when you can be perceived on top of it?
- Register your name.com. Go to www.obtainyourname.com or some name registration site, and register your name as fast as you can. Register your kids' names, too.
- Dedicate time to make it happen. Or it won't happen. If you want to make a lasting mark, it must be preceded with a master plan.
- Get others to help you. List the people you think can help you or help you connect—and ask for their support. (The easiest way to get support? Give it first—without keeping score.)

- Stay in front of the people you want to do business with. By combining your outreaches, you can create a steady flow of your images (in the paper, weekly e-zine, on TV, your newsletter, etc.) to your target market. It takes between five and ten images to create awareness great enough to make a buying decision.
- Become a resource. It's much more powerful than someone perceiving you as a salesman or entrepreneur. People will want to be around you and pay attention to what you say; if they believe what you say and do has value to them and their business.
- Persistence and consistency are the secrets. Don't do anything once—and then sit back and wait. You must keep plugging without expectation. If you're good, have patience. Your phone will ring.
- Ignore idiots and zealots. There are a lot of jealous people and naysayers in the world. Ignore them. People who rain on your parade have no parade of their own.
- Become known as a person of action. The result of these actions will be a person who is known for getting things done—a leader. It's not just a reflection of you—it's a reflection on your company, the products and services you offer, and your personal brand."

Jeanne Bice is a great example of personal branding. Jeanne doesn't just sell her Quacker Factory apparel on QVC—she also sells herself. She has created a community of women who have become loyal to her and her brand, who are part of Jeanne's circle of friends. Part of this brand-building has been creating joyous rituals, like suggesting that a woman "quack" when she recognizes another woman wearing one of her sweaters! She has also hosted "Quacker Cruises" where she and her customers vacation together. By creating these rituals, among others, she has developed a cultish loyalty to her brand. If you tune into QVC and watch the Jeanne Bice hour, you'll regularly hear call-ins from her customers/fans who profess their love to Jeanne on air!

Jeanne may have created these rituals intuitively rather than strategically, but it's a great example of building brand loyalty through a sense of belonging.

With The Grocery Game, Teri Gault has also created that sense of belonging. Members call themselves "gamers" and there is a true sense of community on the site—a "we're all in this together" mentality. There are message boards where gamers can chat and share information, and a monthly "Savings Story" that features an individual in the community.

Deann Murphy didn't build her company brand—instead, she built strong product brands that stood on their own, including the Yarn Crafter, Sequin Art, and the BeDazzler. In addition, she created a "world" around each of these products to support sales.

"We started with one item that was unique, a tool like the Yarn Crafter. Then we would build things around that tool—we'd give it kits, we'd give it books, we'd give it accessories—and that made a program," Deann explained. "That also gave us a lot of profitability, because oftentimes the accessories would be more profitable."

MILLION-DOLLAR SECRET

"Branding is so key," said Tomima Edmark, creator of TopsyTail and now www.herroom.com and www.hisroom.com, Internet-based undergarment retail stores. She explains that in a commodity-based business like hers, it's critical to differentiate your company in a way that goes beyond advertising. For herroom.com, Tomima herself is the brand's strength—the expert providing advice on what to choose and how to wear it.

Brands can be built in other ways as well, by projecting and connecting on any number of levels. If we take cars as an example of how different brands connect in different ways, for instance, we can illustrate how products connect on a more visceral, emotional level. It might be the promise of gracious living and admiration (Mercedes), the promise of high performance (BMW), or the promise of "cool" (Volkswagen).

The main idea I'm trying to convey here is that (1) your brand is much more than the look of your logo, (2) you must build your brand on an emotional level to stand out in the marketplace, and (3) you should be as creative as you like in doing so!

THE INSIDE STORY

Maxine Clark

Maxine Clark is an excellent role model for using creativity to build a beloved brand . . . and an extremely successful company in the process.

She founded Build-A-Bear Workshop, Inc., in 1997—a retailer that enables children to build and customize their own stuffed animals. From her 20+ years as an executive in various retail positions (including over three years as president of Payless Shoe Source), she fully understood the power of merchandising, marketing, and product development—and harnessed that power to create a vision for Build-A-Bear Workshop.

The strength of the Build-A-Bear brand lies in the emotional connection between the child and the stuffed animal—as well as the bonding experience between the child and the caregiver as they go through the creative process. Build-A-Bear Workshop (www.buildabear.com) goes far beyond the typical store-bought stuffed animal, which is why the company and the brand have touched the hearts of so many children and grown so quickly.

Maxine talks about her experience in becoming an entrepreneur.

"If it's successful, it has a life of its own. And if you have this vision, when you get X then you want Y, and then you want Z. And that's a good thing. That means there's growth and potential," Maxine explains.

"I think that the misconception that people have is that they're going to be in charge of their destiny," she says. "But if you're really dedicated to your business, your destiny is your consumer, your associates, and the mission you are on."

Today, there are nearly 300 Build-A-Bear Workshop stores worldwide, including company-owned stores in the United States, Canada, and the United Kingdom and franchised stores in Europe, Asia, and Australia. Another of Maxine Clark's additions to entertainment retail is friends 2B made®, which launched in 2004. It's based on the simple premise that kids, especially girls, love dolls.

Her inspiring and informative book, *The Bear Necessities of Business: Build a Company with Heart* (Wiley & Sons, Inc., 2006), is available in bookstores nationwide.

MAKING THE SALE

You've got your position. You've begun building your brand. You've decided how to structure the business. The next step is making the sale.

To help you start thinking about the sales process, here are some basic principles. They'll help you take control of your business and overcome rejection—make you feel, in fact, like you're doing the Tango, arm-in-arm with your buyers *and* going in the same direction!

GENEROSITY PAYS OFF

Most women are used to giving—of their time, their experience, their knowledge, and their wisdom. And if you're a giver, you also know that it generally comes back to you. The same goes in business.

Generosity pays off with consumers, retail buyers, distributors, vendors, and just about anyone else that works with you. If you give without expecting to receive anything in return, you will receive more than you ever expected. For example, out of her personal wish to support uniformed officials, Madelyn Alfano has always offered all uniformed officials in the entire Los Angeles area 50 percent off of her already generous platters of food at her Maria's Italian Kitchen restaurants. It is now a known fact around the Los Angeles area that Maria's Italian Kitchen takes care of its uniformed officials. Nothing is more powerful than word of mouth and Madelyn's generosity spread quickly.

"When you do something for somebody else, you're the one who really gets the gift," says Terrie Williams. She is clearly referring to the gratification of helping others. However, this also tends to come back in other ways. Due to the success of her inspiring books, Terrie Williams often receives letters from prisoners. Inspired by her philosophy regarding humanity and her desire to "recycle inspiration" she answers every letter in some way, even if just to share inspirational information. As she was promoting one of her books at a book-signing event, an employee of the bookstore approached her holding a letter she had written to him in prison. And then he shared an interesting fact. "He was the one who had recommended to the event planner that I do a signing at that store."

When Maria Sobrino first began making her gelatins (from scratch in her kitchen), she couldn't get anyone to buy them—even the small mom-and-pop shops in her target market. Instead of giving up or eating the cost, she believed in her product and offered it to these same stores on a consignment basis, which means they'd only pay her if the gelatins sold. The strategy worked, and her desserts were an instant hit. The very same day she was getting re-orders. In just a few months, brokers were calling with orders as large as 1,000 cases, for which she then began charging upfront.

Don't be limited by constraints of convention either. There are numerous ways to market your product or service effectively and economically. On her way to financial success, Terrie Williams used several approaches I truly admire. "I put postcards, fliers, whatever, wherever I am—taxis, bathroom stalls, movie theaters, doctors' offices. I've gotten calls from people who saw the flier in the back of a taxi, and that's what it's for."

TURN REJECTION INTO AN OPPORTUNITY

If you hear "no thanks" from the person you're trying to sell to, don't give up. "No" may mean "no" now, but it doesn't have to mean "no" forever! In fact, use this as a learning opportunity, and ask a few questions before you hang up the phone or leave the store. It is important to gather feedback so that you can learn if there are any issues that need correcting. Following are some of the questions I ask:

- Would you consider buying my product or using my services at another time?
- If not, why not?
- What would need to change?
- If the timing is not right, when would be a good time for me to call you again? May I contact you then?
- Is there anything that you would change about the product or packaging that would improve it?
- After I've made the changes you suggest, may I send you a sample for your feedback?
- Are there any other companies or people you could recommend where my product would be a fit?

Not only will you get important information by asking such questions, but you are also building a relationship with the buyer.

MAKE IT EASY FOR PEOPLE TO BUY FROM YOU

No matter what you are selling, it is important to make it easy for people to buy merchandise or services from you. For instance, my company sells wholesale to retailers—stores who sell directly to end users. At my first trade show, I went in selling my first product, TP Savers, in 48-unit boxes. However, I quickly learned that retailers wanted 6- to 12-unit increments! Smaller independent stores purchase in smaller quantities because they don't want to be stuck with a lot of excess inventory—and they often don't have the storage capacity. This was important information. It meant a few extra cents to me per box, but selling in smaller increments was essential to make it easy for them to buy.

GET THE TOOLS YOU NEED

Two essential tools you need to make sales easier are a merchant account at a bank, which allows you to accept credit cards, and an eCommerce account, which allows you to take payments online. Both of these are essential to getting up and running before you can begin selling.

GETTING THE WORD OUT

Part of strengthening your sales is creating awareness and demand from end users. Paid advertising is one way, with countless options that we will leave to the many books on effective advertising. But there's one economical way that I've found highly effective—that is, through public relations. When your target market sees your product in a magazine or learns about your unique offering on TV, via the Internet, or in a local paper or newsletter, you create "pull"—they'll seek out your product or service for themselves.

PUBLIC RELATIONS: THE *FREE* MEDIA IS YOUR FRIEND!

Since launching my company, I've had the good fortune of appearing on over 100 television and radio shows nationwide. From the *Today* show to *Good Morning America* to *CNN* to the *Wall Street Journal* and *People* magazine, these media appearances and placements have given my company an enormous boost.

THE ROLE OF A PUBLICIST

I am often asked, "Do I need a publicist?" The answer is "it depends." If you follow these guidelines, there is no reason why you can't pitch a story yourself. However, publicists offer established relationships with contacts, knowledge of media, and expertise in selling stories. In addition, you have many aspects of the business to manage and publicity is time consuming. So if it is in your budget, a publicist can be a useful consultant.

One cautionary note: if your story has not been crafted to be interesting, even the best publicist will not be able to secure air time or print placement. To find a publicist, ask for recommendations from others in your industry or local business contacts.

So, the question is, how do *you* take advantage of the free media? If this is part of your strategy (and it may not be right for every business) then first you need to adopt a media mindset.

What is a media mindset? Put yourself in the shoes of media companies. Understanding that the media needs stories—in fact, their business depends on stories—is your first step. Rather than be intimidated and believe they won't be interested in you and your product, look at it from their perspective—TV news now needs to fill 24 hours a day with programming, magazines need fresh information from cover to cover, and newspapers need updated content on a daily basis. In other words, they need you!

CRAFT YOUR STORY

Of course, the media needs you to be *interesting*. Consider it from the perspective of a TV producer or journalist—while very exciting to you, the fact that you have a new, terrific product is probably not newsworthy in and of itself. And because they're very busy, you need to tell them exactly why it is newsworthy. Pique their interest and give them a reason to interview you with a compelling story or unusual angle. Does your product make children safer at a time when safety is getting a lot of coverage, like Julie Clark's The Safe Side? Does it have a quirky and unique angle, like Karen Belasco's giant, personalized fortune cookies? The answer isn't the same for every business. Only you can determine what makes your company newsworthy.

PROVIDE EXPERTISE

Becoming an expert on a topic is a good way to interest the media. That doesn't mean reading 50 books and then calling yourself an expert, though. Talk about something you already do! For example, I manufacture Mom Invented™ products. I do this every day, which means I can speak about inventing from experience and the mistakes I've made.

Do some brainstorming. If you sell a product, can you claim expertise in some area? Rachel Ashwell, who founded Shabby Chic, basically grew up in flea markets—her parents were antique collectors. She turned this into a business, and her expertise led to writing books, appearing on her own TV show, and being positioned as the authority in her field.

Also, remind the media about your expertise at key times. For example, if you own a chocolate company, remind the media that you're available as a "source" for, say, Valentine's Day or Easter stories. You can even go one step further and give them an angle—a new study that shows why chocolate is good for your health, perhaps, or information on this year's trends.

Tips or "lessons learned" are also a great way to pitch your story. It's a great tool for producers and reporters in a few ways: they can use the exact tips or turn them into questions to ask on air. They like the succinct, helpful information . . . and you'll appreciate knowing what you'll be asked. Whenever a reporter or producer requests an interview now, I forward my own list of "tips" without even being asked—and they almost always use them.

MAKE THE PITCH

Once you have an angle, then you need to "pitch" it to the appropriate media. This can be the most daunting part of getting the word out—calling a reporter or producer and "selling" your story. The first step is to be sure you're contacting the correct person—you don't want to pitch your lifestyle story to the business editor, for example.

Then, it's crucial that you are clear and get to the point quickly; these are busy, deadline-driven people who don't waste time. It also helps to be flexible. For example, I recently included alternative angles when pitching a story—with the hope that if one angle didn't work, another would. In addition, when I speak to or e-mail a reporter, I have learned to ask right away what angle they have in mind for the story. That way, I can alter my story to fit their needs if that makes sense. Obviously, your story needs to be truthful.

DO PRESS RELEASES WORK?

Many people I meet believe that a good press release is essential to getting a write-up in the media. That may be effective if you are announcing your new cure for some disease. But frankly, I don't think the media can digest the shear number of press releases sent out, much less spend the time necessary deciphering the real news from the non-real. That said, I think press releases are still useful, but for a different audience. A release can be very effective, if professionally crafted, when sent to other key people such as customers (or prospective customers), investors, or other industry influencers. In addition, the press release may be posted on the Internet and provide people searching the Internet with another way to find you, your company, or your product.

SELL THE SIZZLE!

Hopefully, your efforts will lead to an interview. No matter what the media—print, online, TV, or radio—be sure to take full advantage of the opportunity! For some, this comes easily. Jeanne Bice, for instance, has always been in the public eye—she even had her own radio show long before launching her business. For others, though, it can be intimidating. Even those who feel comfortable being interviewed can miss the mark.

For example, I once invited a woman to appear with me on a TV segment because I thought her company and product would be a perfect complement. While she was fantastic presenting herself and demonstrating her product, she forgot to mention where customers could buy it. Her potential customers saw her on TV, but her sales were not impacted. This is an important lesson: you need to plan ahead to make the most of the opportunity!

That means preparation. And even if you seek the help of media coaches, the bottom line is that you are the one performing when the media calls. You can hire people to do just about any other aspect of your business, except for your public presentation to the world. Let's look at the advantages of each media type, and what you can do to prepare for each kind.

TELEVISION

The beauty of television is that it allows you to personally connect with your target audience, who can "get to know you." A live studio audience can add another level of connection as well. When I did a Seattle talk show, called *Northeast Morning* before a live studio audience, I found it exhilarating to view the audience's reaction. It gave me an opportunity to "feel" the responses of real people, which doesn't happen in a regular TV news studio setting. Regardless of the audience, however, the key is to be prepared:

- **Speak in sound bites.** Sound bites are short, concise, interesting statements. Most TV segments last only one to four minutes, so it's important to know exactly what you want to say. It must work for you or it is not worth it. Before going on the air, establish one to three key points you want to convey and come up with language that succinctly communicates these points.

Julie Clark, who was thrust quickly into the public eye with the success of her first company, Baby Einstein, said that although public exposure is scary at first, practice makes perfect. "You start getting your answers down and you know what you're doing," Julie explains.

Kathy Gendel, founder of Breezies® Intimates—sold exclusively on TV through QVC—felt the same way when she first started out. "The words would not even come," says Kathy. "I was like a deer in headlights." Now she's a veteran talker who's a natural, and she's used the power of talk to build a multi-million dollar business today.

MILLION-DOLLAR SECRET

"Treat the camera as your best friend," says Kathy Gendel. "Speak to it as you would speak to your friend."

- **Know what you're in for.** Most reporters or TV hosts will ask a gamut of questions—about your company, products, services, and you personally. Be prepared and don't be shy. Ask the producer or reporter in advance the theme of the segment, and find out what types of information they're seeking from you. By knowing in advance what they want, you won't be surprised and you'll fulfill the needs of the segment producer. In fact, if you know what they are looking for, you may be able to provide them with important questions or facts. Adding value to a show becomes a win-win for both of you and good guests nearly always get invited back!

- **Prepare for the tough stuff.** No matter how much you know in advance, every once in a while you'll get a zinger—one of those questions you hate to answer! How can you prepare for this? Imagine every possibility, come up with possible questions yourself, and rehearse the answers.

  For instance, I am commonly asked how much money my company makes in a year. While this is a legitimate question, I keep such information proprietary. Instead, I answer by sharing information that plugs the success of my products, like "We had a great year last year and are forecasting growth of 100 percent."

- **Be gracious.** Don't be lured in by the raunchy elements of today's reality shows. Instead, be gracious, polite, and dignified. You are on television and therefore hundreds, thousands, and even millions are watching your every move! The old adage about "first impressions" is true, so do your best to present yourself well—for your own sake and for your family's.

- **Dress the part.** For TV, appearance is critical. And although it doesn't mean you need to spend a lot on your wardrobe, you do need to consider carefully what you'll wear. I've worn my own clothes, borrowed outfits from family members, and even bought a jacket for $18 that I wore on KTLA *Los Angeles Morning News*. What they all had in common is that they conveyed the right look with the right colors. Colors that work well on TV include red, blue, and black; white is never a good idea. Make sure to wear solids rather than patterns. Although people like Oprah do wear jeans on occasion, wearing jeans is rarely a good idea (unless you *are* Oprah!).

Although it can seem like a lot of preparation, remember that TV can be an awesome marketing tool for your business. For Teri Gault, time spent traveling to make local TV appearances has really paid off. Although much of her company's growth has been through word of mouth—friends referring friends—local TV has also helped. She gives an example of one specific appearance she made in Colorado.

"Their consumer reporter is very well respected. The guy is really objective and is a critical thinker and he blows the top off things that are scams," Teri explains. "All of a sudden our Colorado franchisees had 6,000 orders in an hour."

RADIO

The advantage of radio is that people listen to what you are saying—they're not distracted by, say, your shoes or your body language. The disadvantage is that they can't see you, so it's harder to connect with your audience. As with TV, however, it is still critical to prepare interesting, snappy sound bites. If it's not a live, in-studio interview—radio interviews are frequently conducted over the phone—it can be a challenge to keep your energy up. So be sure to sit up straight with both feet on the ground, lean forward and smile as you speak. I truly believe that this smile comes across, and that your physical posture will help you stay focused and to keep your energy flowing.

PRINT MEDIA

While television and radio are powerful, they are fleeting. People have to be watching or listening during those exact minutes that you happen to be on the air. Magazines can be a fantastic medium because people keep them around, often for a month or longer. They are circulated at business offices, libraries, cafés, and also offer the opportunity to share product photos, so customers will recognize it later on the store shelves.

Karen Belasco's business was launched on the success of a media placement in a woman's magazine 11 years ago. "We were featured in the magazine, and then all of a sudden I had to have an 800 number," says Belasco. "I set one up in my parents' house, and we took orders day and night. The next thing I knew I had a business!"

It was only a year ago when she began to pay for advertising—for the first 10 years she relied on free media placements like these, plus word of mouth.

Newspapers are another key type of print media. Because of their role of reporting "news," newspapers tend to have a high degree of credibility. This can be an important factor for some companies— a business-to-business venture, for instance, in which you're providing a service to the business world. Plus, most newspapers come out daily, which means that they have an enormous demand for news stories.

SPECIALTY MEDIA: INFOMERCIALS, INTERNET, PODCASTS, AND BLOGS

As our world has become increasingly hungry for information, and technology has blossomed to satisfy this demand, an almost endless array of new opportunities for media exposure is available ranging from self-purchased infomercials to blogs, podcasts, and streaming videos.

With her new company, The Safe Side, Julie Clark tried something different—a commercial with a direct-response company. It's basically an extended-length commercial with an 800 number and Web site enabling viewers to order product immediately. While it may not have been the most effective method for another product—even her Baby Einstein videos—she found it was highly effective in getting the word out about The Safe Side. Plus, she knew TV would help leverage the already well-established visibility of her business partner, John Walsh—host of the TV show "America's Most Wanted." Her strategy worked!

Of course, anyone who's ever watched TV remembers Tomima Edmark's spot for the TopsyTail. By buying time and airing one of three spots—which ranged in length from 30 seconds to 2 minutes— the power of TV showed how easy TopsyTail was to use, and made her product an instant success. The fact that people could call an 800 number to order it was also a contributing factor.

BLOOPERS AND MISTAKES: LEARNING THE HARD WAY

One of my appearances on *Good Morning America* didn't go as well as I had hoped. (It's one of those moments I've re-played in my mind again and again.) So what happened? As always, I prepared. The writer for the show segment called me the day before the show to discuss what I planned to say. I offered her some key points and she told me what they hoped to achieve with the segment and I felt confident. In the excitement of the actual segment, my nerves kicked in, and for a split second I lost my train of thought. Rather than just take a breath and pause to gather my thoughts (which no one would have even noticed), I made a face and rolled my eyes on national television! Oh, how I wished I could have taken that nanosecond back.

So I decided to learn from my mistake and get it right the next time. As it turned out, it was much worse for me than anyone else . . . and *Good Morning America* invited me back.

IT'S A WRAP

So . . . what do all this positioning, structuring, branding, and publicizing have in common? First, that it's important to have a unique vision for your company—and a plan for how to best communicate it. Second, that there are no holds barred when it comes to creativity—let your ideas flow, like so many of our Millionaire Moms did, and see where they'll take you. While you can learn from their examples and adopt some of their strategies, there are no rules to follow. In fact, the more creative you are the more competitive your company may be. That's what "businesses without borders" is all about!

In the next chapter, we talk about finding the much-needed funding to help get you off the ground, and creating ongoing cash flow to keep the business going and growing.

Money Matters:
Raising Capital

Most entrepreneurs don't have the luxury of unlimited funding to start and grow their businesses. In fact, many of them become entrepreneurs to find a way to make money while doing something they love. Or, they find themselves needing to make a living when the "right job" has eluded them.

This chapter will provide information and tools to help you find the money you need to fund and grow your business. Whether the "seed" money you need is a few hundred dollars or a few hundred thousand, I'll offer strategies that will help make your company more likely to receive funding, and offer ideas on exactly where you can find it. I will also provide specific examples from our Millionaire Moms, who funded their businesses in a variety of creative ways.

DIALING FOR DOLLARS
First, raising money is not easy. However, nearly every entrepreneur needs money at some point, so don't be ashamed that you need it to get your company off the ground or to grow to the next level! Despite the inclination of reporters to highlight entrepreneurs who hit it big

from the start, in my experience few businesses are immediate successes. It normally takes time, money, occasional sleepless nights, and humility to grow a business.

Like product development, marketing, and sales, raising money is an important task. And it's an ongoing task—it doesn't end once you've launched your business and start making sales. Money is usually necessary for capital expenditures like equipment, space, manufacturing, and marketing. In fact, one of the ironies can be rather surprising: you suddenly have strong sales, but need even more money to handle your new production requirements. Even companies that seem well established can continue for years on somewhat shaky financial ground, carefully timing expenditures around income.

In the early days of my company I appeared on a national TV show to demonstrate my newest products. Anyone watching would have been surprised to know that immediately after the segment I found I didn't have enough credit on my card to pay for a simple lunch! Every dollar I made went into funding the company's growth. And that didn't leave much for any "extras"—even lunch! And, in my opinion, I was succeeding.

It's a paradox. As a leader, the entrepreneur must portray an image of financial security in the face of periodic financial insecurity—or in some instances, financial terror! Everyone wants to back a winner, and that can be the greatest irony of all.

"I've had so many people say to me 'you have such a charmed life,'" says Kathy Gendel of Breezies® Intimates. "Nothing is charming about possibly losing your house! During those years of blood, sweat, and tears, I wore my poker face." Kathy never lost her house, but the threat lingered during the early stages of her business, when it functioned as her primary source of collateral.

Nell Merlino of Count Me In agrees. Her nonprofit provides micro-loans to women in business so she witnesses the entrepreneurial process, each step of the way. "There's a lot of smoke and mirrors and fantasy that goes along with being an entrepreneur," explains Nell.

MILLION-DOLLAR SECRET

You will need money to start and grow your business, and nobody is going to raise it for you. "The reality is that somebody has to help you initially," said Lane Nemeth, who started with nothing before building Discovery Toys. "You just have to do enough research."

FIRST STEPS FOR FUNDING

If you plan to ask anyone to help fund your business—whether it's a friend, family member, bank, or venture capitalist—it is essential to have a written plan. This plan is different from the business plan you created in Chapter 2, although having both is ideal. This new plan—your financial plan—will include detailed information about your costs, revenues, and profit model, with current information and forecasts for the future.

Having both these plans in place is important for your own purposes—to help you figure out, as a businessperson, where the company is going and how much capital you'll need. The financial plan becomes absolutely critical when you begin seeking outside funding. That's because banks and potential investors will need to understand that you are thorough, thoughtful, serious, and have sufficient financial skills to justify handling their money. In addition, they need to see that you are willing to invest your own time and money.

Unfortunately, many businesspeople do not prepare enough. I frequently encounter blank expressions when I ask businesswomen about their one-year or three-year plans. But experts say it's absolutely essential to have such plans.

"You wouldn't have a wedding without a plan. There are a lot of things you wouldn't do without a pretty comprehensive plan," explains Nell Merlino of Count Me In. She explains that the more clarity a business owner has, the better.

"It's a mistake to go to somebody and say 'I need $50,000' or 'I need $5,000,'" says Nell. "Tell me what you're going to do with it. Is it $2,000 for marketing and $3,000 for inventory? Just what is it?"

Your plan will help determine these answers. It will pull together the following: your current "financials," including an income statement (a.k.a. profit and loss or P&L statement), cash flow statement, and balance sheet (described in detail in Chapter 6). You will also need a forecast that estimates your business's potential future growth. Standard bookkeeping software packages such as Quick Books® automatically produce financial reports (the income, cash flow, and balance sheet statements).

Karen Belasco admittedly built Good Fortunes without a solid plan. Nevertheless, she stressed the importance of developing one. "If I didn't have family help, I probably would have been out of business 20 times," Karen explained. "Budgets and forecasts and plans for growth—all very important. Did I have any of them? No. Would it have made a big difference? I think a huge difference."

Those who did have solid plans in place seemed to achieve their success more quickly and with fewer setbacks.

Take Kathy Gendel. She founded Breezies® with a detailed, well-thought-out three-year plan and pursued investors right from the onset. Her plan worked. In just 12 years, she's grown the company into a multi-million dollar business and into a well-loved brand on QVC.

MILLION-DOLLAR SECRET

"An entrepreneurial business is not a business where you can wing it or just fly by the seat of your pants," said Kathy Gendel. *"If you've got a lot of money, everyone wants to give you money. If you don't have any money, no one wants to give you a dime. Always plan for those rainy days."*

So what's the first step in creating a plan?

"The sooner you put down what you know, the sooner you'll find out what you don't know," explains Nell Merlino. That said—the best thing to do is just get started.

If you already have financial and accounting know-how, great—you're one step ahead. However, if you're like the rest of us, you may want to seek outside help. There are accounting and bookkeeping firms you can hire for assistance. And, for someone with the drive and stamina to work and learn, there are many outstanding free and low-cost resources available:

- The Small Business Administration (SBA), through its Small Business Development Centers located throughout the country (www.sba.gov).
- Service Corps of Retired Executives (SCORE) provides free mentoring from experienced businesspeople; local chapters are located nationwide (www.score.org).
- Find micro-loan and support services—see www.microenterpriseworks.org.
- Local business organizations—Chambers of Commerce and organizations such as the National Association of Women Business Owners (NAWBO) will often be able to refer suitable mentors (www.nawbo.org).
- Local colleges with accounting, business, or entrepreneurship departments.
- Fellow entrepreneurs.
- Senior-level people at local community banks.
- Numerous useful Web sites. For a list of such sites, log in to: www.mominventors.com/millionairemoms.

In Chapter 6, we also include sample financial documents to help you, including samples of an income (profit and loss) statement, a cash flow statement, and a balance sheet.

SOURCES OF FUNDING

So now that you know the importance of organizing your financial information and building a financial plan, it's time to figure out exactly where you're going to get that funding!

START WITH YOURSELF

Before you can expect anyone else to invest in your business, plan to "bootstrap," and invest your own money first. This will help clarify your direction as well as legitimize you to the outside world. But if you're already stretched thin financially, where can you turn? Here are a few simple but workable ideas:

- **Use what you have.** If you have even a little money saved, now may just be that "rainy day" you've been waiting for. For instance, Victoria Knight-McDowell and her husband, Rider, launched Airborne with personal funds, primarily the proceeds from a television screenplay that Rider sold to a Hollywood studio.
- **Cut corners in your everyday life.** What can you do without? A $20-a-month magazine subscription will cost you $240 per year. Or, cut out a $3-per-day expense—one coffee latte—and you just saved over $700 per year! Dig up five "cuts" like this and you can quickly free up several thousand dollars—enough to pay for a prototype, brochure, trade show booth, Web site, consulting hours, etc.
- **Become a better shopper.** We recently saved $500 just by re-shopping our home fire insurance. The biggest savings we've found is through buying groceries. The more we spend on groceries, the more we save each month because that means we are eating IN!
- **Stretch your current work situation.** Stay in your current job as long as possible, and if you can, earn overtime or extra money. Then, use your evenings and free time to build the business—a small sacrifice for creating a long-term life change.

This is what Tomima Edmark did. Dissatisfied with her corporate job and frustrated by the "glass ceiling," she wanted to do something else with her life. Instead of quitting in frustration, however, she meticulously planned how to develop her invention, TopsyTail®, while continuing to earn an income. She also took on another job to come up with the extra money she needed to pay for the TopsyTail injection mold, using her free time to write a book on kissing (!), which she then sold to a major publishing house. She continued working evenings and weekends to make TopsyTail into a successful venture. The strategy worked—she made millions, which she then used to fund her current ventures: HerRoom (www.herroom.com) and HisRoom (www.hisroom.com), online retail stores. "I fund myself," say Tomima. "Men are shocked that my seed capital was me."

- **Stretch personal savings and business revenue.** Spend as little as possible and spread it out over time. Before buying anything, first figure out if it can be financed, making partial payments over time rather than paying in full upfront. (Of course, do watch for unreasonable interest charges and fees.)

GET A PERSONAL LOAN

Another way to come up with money, prior to approaching banks or outside investors, is by securing a personal loan. For instance, you may be able to borrow from your personal retirement plan. More common methods of securing personal finances are:

- **Mortgages.** You can borrow from a lender by leveraging your house. Many of the Millionaire Moms in this book took out second and even third mortgages to fund their businesses. The benefit of these loans is that they are secured by your house, so many lenders are willing to competitively bid on these, and interest rates are relatively low. Plus these loans are generally available quickly, (e.g., about two weeks) and the interest is tax deductible.

- **Credit cards.** Despite some warnings by financial advisors, credit cards are a widely used source of funding. The high interest rates and risk to your personal credit ratings are the main reasons for the skepticism, but frankly, the decision to become an entrepreneur is rife with risk. If you do go this route, do it in a smart way. Secure a card with the lowest possible interest rate, or transfer your debt to your credit card with the lowest rate.

DEBT—A DIFFERENT POINT OF VIEW

Rather than viewing entrepreneurial financial debt with fear, see it as an investment in yourself. Reframing it this way will help you view it as a positive rather than a negative. It's like having a college loan—even if you're still paying it off 10 years after graduation, you probably still consider it a worthy investment.

- **Borrow from family and friends.** This can be a great source of funding because your "investors" will base their decisions on what they know about you personally—and their affection and respect for you—rather than the formal requirements that more institutional lenders will require. Plus, they tend to lend at low or zero percent interest rates. Keep in mind, though, that while some family and friends are completely nonjudgmental, once some people "give" you money they may feel they have license to offer opinions on what you are doing.

Lane Nemeth borrowed $50,000 from her brother-in-law to fund Discovery Toys, and Karen Belasco borrowed $5,000 from each of three family members to get Good Fortunes off the ground. I, too, have borrowed money from family members. In the early days of our business, one of my most exciting moments was receiving our first big purchase order—a retailer had ordered 60,000 units. After those initial joyful moments, we quickly realized that we needed to fund the costs of the manufacturing run, the freight forwarding from overseas, distribution to our warehouse, and shipment to the retailer. (Unfortunately, retailers don't typically pay for orders in advance!) In other words, we needed a sizeable amount of money in a big hurry . . . and we had already tapped into other sources of funding like credit cards and personal savings. Fortunately, I have a big extended family including many generous members who believe in me!

"I stayed at Essence for six months after I resigned. I was asked to remain on staff in order to identify and train my successor, and that also helped me to save money," says Terrie Williams, president and founder of The Terrie Williams Agency. "My mother was also a huge supporter. She helped fund at various levels when retainers weren't coming in a timely fashion, so that's how I did it."

GET CREATIVE WITH BUSINESS FINANCING
There are other ways to fund your business that may be less obvious but can help stretch your cash flow once you're already established.

- **Develop vendor credit.** Try to get your vendors to buy into your idea, and ask if you can pay them over a period of time. This can be a win-win situation in the sense that you will get the inventory or resources you need, while they'll get your business. Be sure to set terms you expect to meet, in order to keep your relationship and reputation intact. Be forthright and if a payment is going to be late tell vendors when they can expect to be paid. This will help foster solid partnerships.

Good Fortunes' Karen Belasco has long relied on her vendors' goodwill. They regularly gave her extensions on payments, which allowed her to retain some working cash flow and stay in business. Even today she'll get extended terms during her busy seasons—

Christmas and Valentine's Day—when she needs to buy so much inventory so far in advance.

"It's really important to get to know your vendors," Karen says. "Know them and know who they are. They should have an investment in you as much as you should have an investment in them."

- **Trade services.** In exchange for a much-needed service—say, engineering expertise or legal advice—an entrepreneur could provide a small percentage of company ownership. This is kind of like bartering. Of course, be wary of giving away too much of your company for the service provided. For example, say you need an engineer to create Computer-Aided Design (CAD) drawings of your prototype. This would probably cost a few thousand dollars, depending on the complexity. But if you offer 10 percent of your future earnings, and your company grows to make millions per year, those initial CAD drawings become very expensive indeed.

Julie Clark had plenty of money to invest into her new company, The Safe Side, after selling Baby Einstein to Disney. However, she still gave 10 percent of the company to The Safe Side's writer. "It will be a lot for a writer, but I also feel like I wouldn't have done it without her involvement," said Clark. "I value that writing to such a great degree that it's worth it."

Debi Davis also exchanged percentages of her company ownership for much-needed services. When restructuring Fit America MD, she added a software diagnostic tool for fitness clubs to use as part of the company's offering. She brought a highly reputable and skilled programmer on board to write the program. She couldn't afford to hire him by the hour, so instead she gave him a percentage of the company. She did the same for her marketing and finance experts, and it has worked out well for her.

Large companies often do something similar—they grant stock options (the right to buy company stock at what may be a below-market price) to employees, thus giving them a potential ownership stake in the company and even more incentive to help the company succeed.

- **Tap into your customers for cash flow.** By working with them in different ways, your customers can be a great source of capital. For instance, we always offer our smaller customers (primarily retailers) a 5 percent discount for prepayment. Since they intend to pay anyway, they might as well earn an extra 5 percent for paying upfront. We gain access to the cash immediately and we have no future administrative burden of invoicing and collections.

- **Consider getting a letter of credit.** The next-best scenario to getting cash upfront from a customer may be getting a letter of credit from a customer. A letter of credit is a documented promise that cash is forthcoming. This letter states that they've made an order and will pay upon delivery. You can then use this letter to try to leverage credit from your own vendors, in order to purchase the necessary supplies or services to fulfill an order.

- **Look into "factoring."** This is an option for businesses with receivables (customers who owe money at a future date). For example, if my company ships a containerload of product to a retail store chain, that retailer will pay me anywhere from 30 to 120 days later. If the delay between the time of the order and receiving the cash payment is hindering operations, factoring may be worthwhile. This is how it works: some banks and financial service companies will "buy" your accounts receivable from you, giving you access to the money you're owed right away. In the example above, the "factor" pays me right away and my retailer now pays the "factor." In return, the factoring company earns a percentage of those receivables—anything from 1 to 15 percent. They then collect on the debt. Your banker can introduce you to companies that factor receivables.

- **Leverage any unused space in your work facility.** Leasing or subleasing your unused office or warehouse space can provide you with critical, timely cash flow..

THE INSIDE STORY

Karen Belasco

In 1995, party planner Karen Belasco brought a unique idea to life—giant, personalized fortune cookies dipped in chocolate. She had created them for a party she was planning, with no intention of creating a business around them. However, they were an instant hit. So when a publicist friend offered to help get a media placement for her sweet treats, Karen agreed and soon found herself getting an 800 number and bakery space to meet the demand.

"The next thing I knew, I had a business," Karen said.

She borrowed money from friends and family and turned her idea into something bigger. In addition to phone sales, she started selling wholesale; word of mouth quickly spread, and the company grew rapidly.

Today, Good Fortunes offers many different product lines and also sells direct to consumers through its Web site at www.goodfortunes.com. The company has become "Hollywood's Secret Cookie Company" with an extensive list of celebrities and Hollywood studios as clients. Good Fortunes also has a significant corporate client base.

Through it all, Good Fortunes has remained a family-focused business, and Karen says she couldn't have done it without her family's support—financially and otherwise.

"During busy holidays, my sisters are here, my brother, my

brother-in-law, and my mother—who works the hardest of anybody," said Karen. "She's been here with me until two in the morning for days in a row, year after year."

In addition to family funds, Karen has financed her business in many ways—credit cards, bank lines of credit, lease-to-own equipment, and extended vendor payments.

She thinks the best advice to women starting and financing their own businesses is to plan, plan, plan. "Along the way you never know what's going to come up," said Karen. "I think planning is the key."

SECURE A BUSINESS LOAN

Besides using your personal savings and credit, there are various types of business loans available today. This section covers some of the options available to you, as well as the pros and cons involved with each of them.

SMALL BUSINESS ADMINISTRATION LOANS

There are a lot of misconceptions about the Small Business Administration (SBA) loans. First, a clarification: the SBA is an agency of the U.S. federal government and does not lend money itself. It does support small business owners in obtaining loans from traditional lenders like banks. The SBA gives lenders an incentive to offer small business loans by guaranteeing those loans if the business fails. These loans are still commonly referred to as "SBA loans." In order to get an SBA loan, an entrepreneur must fit the SBA profile and go through the application process.

This is a good option for companies that fit the profile. However, it's still essentially a bank loan with stringent requirements relating to a history of operational success, demonstrable ability to repay the loan, and varying collateral requirements. This can be a great option for companies challenged to grow because they need to purchase new equipment or a facility (collateral) to continue the growth of their production. Keep in mind that the criteria for an SBA loan are not too different from the criteria for standard loans: collateral, a solid business plan with proven revenue, and an ability to repay the loan are essential.

In 1989, Maria Sobrino secured an SBA loan for $1 million to purchase a factory that would enable her to increase production significantly while also maintaining in-house quality control. Access to this money was extremely helpful. Up to that point Maria had funded the business strictly with cash, purchasing everything upfront. She had little access to credit as she had recently emigrated from Mexico. While cash funding worked for a long time—she sold assets and used income from her own personal investments to fund her business along the way—she could not get to the next level of business without the substantial sum she secured via the SBA loan. For a list of banks offering SBA loans, visit www.sba.gov/financing/basics/lenders.html. For additional financial resources visit www.mominventors.com/million airemoms. There are likely to be banks in your own community that participate in this program.

MICRO-LOANS
One type of loan specifically designed for young companies as an alternative to an SBA loan, is referred to as a micro-loan. Although micro-loans are typically much smaller than most SBA loans ($5,000 to $50,000) a micro-loan can be just enough financing to provide working capital and help accelerate early growth. Plus, a good repayment record on a micro-loan can help you demonstrate your creditworthiness for future loans. Micro-loans are sometimes also backed by the SBA.

So where do you find micro-loans? They are increasingly available from multiple sources.

Nell Merlino of Count Me In lends money to women-owned businesses in the form of micro-loans. In fact, Count Me In has a program called Make Mine a $Million Business® program with founding partner OPEN from American Express℠ that offers financing, mentoring, and marketing resources to women who want to grow their businesses to a million dollars in revenue. According to Nell, Count Me In's goal is to get 1 million women entrepreneurs to a million dollars in revenue by 2010.

There are many other organizations that offer micro-loan programs. To find them, visit www.microenterpriseworks.org. Another group offering loans and support in regions throughout the country can be found at www.accionusa.org.

It is essential to invest the time and energy in getting certain elements in place prior to applying for loans, including a sound business plan and realistic financial forecasts. If micro lenders sense you are careless or taking the process lightly, they will not want to risk their money. "It really should embody your marketing plan, your financing plan, your vision, your staffing," explains Nell Merlino. "To really do it right, it tells a whole picture."

OTHER BUSINESS LOANS

Finally, it also may be possible to find people or organizations willing to lend you money based on the interest rate return and/or by securing it with either a personal guarantee or lien on your car or other personal or "real" property. They also may consider loaning you the money with the possibility of converting it to company stock—also called a "convertible bridge loan."

Remember, when it comes to funding it's helpful to have guidelines but there are no set rules. For instance, I recall a planning meeting early on with an SBA counselor. While he offered good information, he also advised me not to start my company until I had six months of reserve funding in the bank. This is good advice. But like all advice, you need to consider it and then apply what is right for your situation. Personally, if I had listened to that particular suggestion, I would never have launched my company! Yes, we took a bigger risk, but somehow we managed to make it work.

OUTSIDE INVESTORS

"I have a great idea and all I need is an investor." This is a common statement by new entrepreneurs. But this statement usually indicates that not enough effort has been put into developing a financial plan. As I've said throughout this chapter, it's best for start-up and early-stage businesses to invest their own "sweat equity" and to bootstrap, searching every other means of funding available before seeking outside investment. That's because (1) it can be challenging to find an outside investor at this stage; (2) they'll typically expect a lot in return for risking their money on a largely untested concept; and (3) the first thing they are likely to ask is, "What have you already invested yourself?" If you haven't demonstrated a willingness to risk your own money or collateral, an investor might wonder—"Why should I?"

Unfortunately, Lane Nemeth learned this the hard way. When she founded Discovery Toys she was in desperate need of money. An investor offered her $90,000 in return for 20 percent of the company. Lane says she realized in hindsight that it was a huge mistake—it was too large a percentage of the company to give away for a relatively small investment, especially once her company grew to $100 million in sales. Only Lane can judge for sure what kind of mistake this was, but from my perspective she did what she had to do and ultimately got out of a hole and built an enormously successful company.

Investors differ from the traditional lenders we discussed earlier in that they essentially become partial owners of your company—owners of "equity" in your company—in exchange for putting their money at risk. A similar example of this kind of investment is the stock market. Individuals or institutions can purchase shares of stock through public offerings and become partial owners.

There is a time and place to seek "equity" investors. And despite Lane Nemeth's experience, she now acknowledges that all investors are not out for blood, and would even consider doing it again, with the right investor. Typically, entrepreneurs in the earliest stages of funding will sell their first "equity," i.e., a piece of their company, to friends and family. Once these sources have been exhausted, they may expand their search to professional investors.

In this section I'll explain the two most common types of outside investors: angel investors (angels) and venture capitalists (also known as VCs). Most entrepreneurs during the early stages will seek out angels—typically wealthy individuals, or groups of individuals, who invest their own money directly into a company. VCs, on the other hand, are professionally managed investment groups that usually focus on businesses with some type of track record or an exceptional growth potential, and will invest larger amounts.

SEEK OUT SUPPORT

It's important to have professional support at the point that you start speaking to serious investors. This is no time to rely on your family estate attorney and bookkeeper to advise you. Experienced professionals will ensure that your corporate documents are accurate and can also better analyze and help present your finances to improve the likelihood of success. Seek out advisors who can help you think about the impact of investment on your ownership—in this investment round as well as in future rounds. To find people who are qualified, ask other local entrepreneurs who have raised capital or ask professional angel investors for recommendations.

ANGEL INVESTORS

In 2005, "angels" invested $23.1 billion in a total of 49,500 entrepreneurial ventures in the United States. In the same year, women represented just 8.7 percent of those seeking angel investments.[1]

---

[1] *The Angel Investor Market in 2005: The Angel Market Exhibits Modest Growth*, Center for Venture Research, Jeffrey Sohl. March 27, 2006.

Although the overall percentage of women seeking funding is still low, the women who did seek funding had a high success rate: a third of the women seeking angel funding actually secured it, higher than the overall success rate. This implies one of two things: that the women seeking funding were better prepared, and/or the angels like women-owned companies. Either way it's a positive sign for women entrepreneurs.

To determine whether or not outside investment is a good option for you, be realistic about the potential returns to the investors. Angel investors will typically expect to earn an exceptionally high return— much greater than they can find with more conservative investment options. Ask yourself if it's realistic to promise this type of return. Think through your growth potential and be thoughtful in estimating the ultimate return your investors are likely to earn.

"Most people shy away from an overly aggressive plan because they know you really can't do it," said Maxine Clark of Build-A-Bear Workshop. "People think you don't know what you're talking about— that you might be too naïve."

Understand that you'll have someone to answer to. Your angel investors—essentially owners—will expect to stay informed and will often want to share their opinions and recommend strategies. If you became an entrepreneur strictly to avoid answering to others, obtaining your funding from outside investors may not be the right option for you.

Ask yourself the following questions, which come from The Angel Capital Education Foundation:

- "Are you ready to give up a certain amount of ownership and control in your company?
- Can you demonstrate that your business will generate significant revenue over the next three to five years, and will produce a return on investment?
- Are you willing to take advice from investors and work with a board of directors whose opinions might differ from yours?

- Do you have an exit plan for yourself or the company?
- Is your product developed and nearing completion?
- Do you have existing or potential customers?
- Have you exhausted other forms of capital, such as your own funds, family, or friends?
- Can you demonstrate that your business will grow to $15 million or more in revenue over the next three to five years?"

Once you've answered these questions and determined that angel investors are a good option, where exactly can you find these angels? These are the most common angel investors:

1. Family and friends;
2. Local community contacts—"friends of friends";
3. People who share a social or demographic profile, such as "women" or "minority" investors, or people who share a similar concern for something (e.g., the environment);
4. People you admire, or know to be in the same or similar industry sector; and finally
5. Organized groups of angel investors.

TO FIND AN ANGEL YOU MIGHT
ASK FOR ADVICE INSTEAD OF MONEY

The key to finding angels in the first four categories is to talk to people. Ask others what they think about your business, and about who might want to offer advice on growing your company. A strategy I often go back to is this advice I once read: "The best way to get money is to ask for advice. The best way to get advice is to ask for money." So do whatever you can to expand your circle of advisors. Many times, these advisors will become your investors!

Although Maria Sobrino didn't start with an advisory board, she's recently realized the value one can offer . . . especially at her current stage of business, as she prepares for additional growth. "For many years, I said I was going to do this all by myself," Maria explained. But she said being a one-woman band can lead to a limited view and mistakes made. So she recently established an advisory board. "They are looking at me, they believe in my company, and now they're helping me go to that next level," explained Maria.

A local business group or a local chapter of the trade association in which your business operates are other potential sources to help you identify prospective angel investors. Introduce yourself and establish relationships. Also, ask your advisors—your attorney, accountant, banker, marketing consultant, financial consultant, even professors—who they recommend you speak to. All these people are likely to have an interest in your success; they also have their own networks and generally want to help.

As the process of raising seed or start-up capital has matured, the sophistication of angel investors has also increased. One result has been a growing population of organized angel "groups." They tend to fit four different models: regionally based (e.g., Sacramento Angels—www.sacangels.org), sector-based (e.g., Life Science Angels—www.lifescienceangels.com), cause-related (Investors Circle—www.investorscircle.net, www.goldenseeds.com), or general (www.keiretsuforum.com) and online posting groups (www.angeldeals.com, www.activecapital.org).

INSIDE ONE ANGEL GROUP

The Keiretsu Forum (www.keiretsuforum.com), North America's largest and fastest-growing angel group operates with two core principles in mind: Great Association and Quality Deal Flow. Founded in San Francisco's East Bay in 2000 by Randy Williams, today Keiretsu Forum has over 500 accredited investor members throughout the Western United States and Canada, as well as new chapters in Barcelona, Spain, Prague, the Czech Republic, and Beijing, China. Since its inception members have invested over $80 million in 128 companies in technology, healthcare/life sciences, consumer products, real estate, and other segments with high growth potential.

The following is a Q&A with Randy Williams:

Question: Randy, you know many "angel investors." Can you describe them?

Randy: A typical angel investor has had a wonderful scorecard in life. This means they have made money. They are entrepreneurs who still have it in their DNA to be a part of robust teams to help companies grow. They may not want to take the risks themselves to create certain companies or may be at an age where they do not want to start over. Nevertheless, they still want to amortize their money and their Rolodex to help companies grow while being part of the company. What motivates my Keiretsu Forum members is that they want to help. They want to be called upon to help a company grow.

Question: What is the role and purpose of an "angel group"?

Randy: I believe the role of an angel group is to provide a platform for members to be better, smarter investors to have superior returns in the private equity market place. But also, our members have the responsibility to give the entrepreneurs the opportunity to grow their companies—not just with capital, but with resources and access to allow that to happen. Additionally, I think it is the responsibility of Keiretsu Forum members to give back to the community. I am proud to say that every year we give back a quarter of a million dollars to local charities. As of this writing, we have given to 68 charities nationwide.

Question: According to statistics, and my own conversations with women, very few seek angel or VC funding. What suggestions do you have for women entrepreneurs considering this path?

Randy: First, are the basics I tell everyone—you need to meet the requirements of having good revenue and profit (or revenue and profit potential), a defined market opportunity, a solid management team, intellectual property, and a reasonable valuation. Second, empathize with the investor. Ask yourself, how am I going to make money for you? Third, ask for things other than money such as advice, introductions, and contacts. Fourth, find a champion. Ask people with expertise in your area for help and try to get them actively involved in your progress and the fund-raising process.

See www.mominventors.com/millionairemoms for a list of angels and directories.

VENTURE CAPITAL

A venture capitalist (VC) differs from an angel investor in the sense that they exist strictly to invest money. VCs are typically more sophisticated organizations (usually organized as limited partnerships) run by professional financial businesspeople—often entrepreneurs themselves—who have pooled investment dollars into a "fund" which can be worth hundreds of millions of dollars. This money typically comes from outside groups and individuals who want to invest, with the help of professional managers, in rapidly growing companies offering the potential of an especially high rate of return (20 to 50 percent per year) within a five- to seven-year time frame. These types of companies generally represent a higher degree of risk than larger, established, slower-growing companies.

The VCs will invest money in several companies that fit their investment criteria such as industry, stage of growth, and strategic plans. It's typically pretty big money—not less than $1 million per investment, and usually over $5 million. They will often assist in the development of new products and services, and seek to add value to a company through active participation.

For start-up and very early-stage companies, venture capital is generally not appropriate. There are additional issues at play for women-owned companies that make venture capital seem more improbable.

"Men invented venture capital as a vehicle for growth. But VCs want to see an exit strategy in three to five years—and many women don't want to commit to cashing out that soon. They want the creativity and passion to go on and on," said Victoria Colligan, founder of the online network Ladies Who Launch in a recent article in *Fortune Small Business*.[2]

In the same article, Springboard Enterprises' Amy Millman said, "We are discouraged from an early age from using the word 'I' too often. That's a problem, because VCs are most interested in hearing the word 'I,' with dollar signs attached. Women will talk about the great team effort, which is a cue to investors that the women are not really the ones in charge or are not the ones who execute."

Despite some of these psychological barriers, women are still making progress and getting VC funding. More organizations exist to help them do so, like Springboard Enterprises (www.springboardenterprises.org) which has matched up women business owners with $3.4 billion of venture capital money as well as the Women's Technology Cluster—the nation's first technology-industry business incubator specifically targeted to women entrepreneurs (www.wtc-sf.org). In addition, it's become increasingly clear in this male-skewed industry that many women-owned businesses are well worth the risk. While not right for most start-ups, I believe that there are cases where venture capital is critical in helping certain kinds of companies beat the competition and make it big.

---

[2] *Fortune Small Business Magazine*, May 1, 2006.

You can dramatically improve your chances of successfully raising venture capital by understanding the basics of the process, as well as learning some of the lingo.

So how do VCs work?

Like angel investors, VCs tend to have market-sector focus areas that can be as general as technology, energy, or consumer goods, or as specific as "business software applications" or "green energy." This is important to note so that you focus on firms that specialize in your area. They also tend to invest at a particular "stage" of growth. The general stages are Seed (prior to the organization of the company), Start-up (also known as Early Stage), Expansion Stage, and Later Stage.

Venture capitalists need to be "sold." That's why preparation is critical when approaching VCs. Most of them review hundreds of business plans before selecting a handful to analyze further, and then a smaller number in which they invest. Therefore, they will not suffer a poor, disorganized presentation that lacks critical information. They will want to see financials like the business planning elements discussed earlier, with plausible forecasts going out three to five years. Your plan should also include:

- A clear explanation of your business concept
- Your proof of concept (evidence that your business concept can be profitably implemented)
- The potential market (the size of the business opportunity in terms of revenues)
- Scalability of your model (how your business model can be expanded)
- The talent, passion, and commitment of the management team
- A three- to five-year exit strategy (which is the strategy to sell or otherwise enable investors to cash out)

VCs may not be for everybody. Karen Belasco of Good Fortunes has been approached herself by venture capitalists . . . but has always turned them down despite her difficulties getting traditional loans.

"They wanted so much of the business that it wasn't going to be my business anymore," explains Karen. "Some of them ask for 50 to 70 percent. It just wasn't worth it for the money they were going to give me."

Lane Nemeth said that a lack of knowledge about venture capitalists was one of her biggest mistakes—and part of the reason why she sold so much of her company for so little. She advises women to deal with them with their eyes wide open.

If you think you'll never be in a position to seek VC money, think again. When I started Mom Inventors, Inc. in early 2003, all I wanted to do was earn enough money to pay off my school loans. I never dreamed of building it into a multi-million dollar business. My viewpoint has since changed radically. For most of the women I interviewed, making millions (some with VC money, some without) wasn't their original goal either—until they learned it was within the realm of possibility.

Here are some things to prepare and watch out for when considering going the venture capital route:

- **Know your stuff.** Start learning about funding sources and the process long before you are desperate. This is the best way to avoid mistakes. Learn how VC investing works. Know your market and your plan and be prepared to present it well.
- **Develop thick skin.** VCs hear many presentations and pride themselves on their ability to dismiss companies for one reason or another (even though some lack grace in delivering their feedback). Treat each "no" as a learning experience and be grateful if you are able to get any information at all in the process. Just like when you're selling any product, remember that it's a numbers game so each "no" is a step closer to a "yes."
- **Understand the dynamics of valuation.** This is a critical part of the investment process. A valuation combines the concept of how much your company is worth and how much money you need to determine what percentage of the company the VC will own. For instance, if you and your VC agree that your company is worth $5 million and you need $6 million to fund your

plan, then the VC will own approximately 55 percent of your company (6MM /11MM = 54.5 percent)—a controlling interest. On the other hand, if you can convince them that your company is worth $20 million, the same $6 million investment would entitle the VC to only 23 percent of your company shares (6MM/26MM = 23 percent) would go to the VC.

- **Understand how to maintain control.** The person or entity who owns 51 percent or more of a company generally has the ability to control the management and direction of the company. Given that the VC is putting substantial capital at risk, it is prudent for them to try to obtain as much control in the company's management as possible. Even when a VC does not own a majority of shares, they will usually require a voting seat on your board of directors and expect to be kept updated on progress. They will also wish to receive regular reports and offer advice to management.

- **Be sure it's a good fit.** You should be interviewing the VC as much as they are interviewing you. Of course, that may be easier said than done, but it will help you avoid mistakes you may later regret. Remember also that a VC is valuable to you not only for the cash they will contribute, but for the doors they can open for you and the substantive expertise that they can bring to the table. Choose wisely!

After Maxine Clark got Build-A-Bear Workshop off the ground with her own initial seed money and the help of her angel investor, it was time to seek out VC money to fund her larger vision. "I invested with people who I felt like I could be friends with, that I could work with every day, that I felt could add value to my business," Maxine explains. "I went with my gut instincts every single time. All the money in the world isn't worth working with somebody who you don't like or don't trust." Her instincts have served her well. In less than 10 years, she's grown Build-A-Bear Workshop into a $350+ million company.

- **Work with an attorney.** Receiving an investment round of venture capital will raise issues related to your corporate structure. It is also a transaction regulated at the state and federal level, specifically by the Securities and Exchange Commission.
- **Prepare to have a board of directors.** Given that you will need to have a corporate entity in place in order to accept funds, you'll be required to have a board of directors responsible for oversight. Large investors will often require a voting seat or seats on your board reflective of their degree of ownership and control.

THE INSIDE STORY

Teri Gault

Former actress Teri Gault and her husband were struggling financially when she decided to launch The Grocery Game in 2000.

"We were very broke," explained Teri. "I was rolling coins at that point to buy groceries."

She was also extremely busy, working three jobs to make ends meet. Despite the lack of funds and lack of time, Teri got creative and managed to stretch both to get the company off the ground. She got an almost-free computer by committing to a two-year Internet service contract, signed up with a Web site hosting company that offered the first three months free, built her own Web site, bought a business license—also with rolled coins—and she was off and running.

Today, TheGroceryGame.com is a multi-million dollar business. It's a unique service that provides members with information on rock-bottom sales at their local grocery stores—matched up with available coupons to help save shoppers 50, 60, even 70 percent off their grocery bills every week. "Teri's List," as it's called, provides info on published and unpublished sales, so that shoppers can save money *and* time once they hit the grocery store. Members, a.k.a. "gamers," describe it as addictive.

Teri is unusual in that she funded her company "organically" over the years—she never borrowed money from anyone, and let her sales fund growth and expenditures.

"It's always been one thing at a time," Teri said. The strategy has worked. Today Teri franchises the Grocery Game by zip code, so it's available in regions across the country. The Grocery Game has over 100,000 members.

© Photo credit: Lindsay Blaker

WHAT IS AN INVESTMENT BANKER?

As your business grows and you begin to look for outside investment or consider selling your company, the term "investment banker" will come up. Since I didn't know what this meant, I wanted to clarify it because it may make sense for your business to work with one.

Lynda Davey is CEO of the Avalon Group (www.avalon-groupltd.com), a boutique investment bank based in New York City. The following interview with her provides insight on the role of an investment banker.

Question: Can you define the term *"investment banker"* and explain what you do?

Lynda: Investment bankers are intermediaries. They either represent a buyer or a seller of companies, or someone who's looking to raise money. So they are not an actual source of funds. A lot of entrepreneurs or people with smaller companies say they don't need an investment banker. What I have found is that the more sophisticated somebody gets, the more they're willing to use an investment banker. If you're bringing in outside money into your company, they can give you advice based on other deals and how they perceive the venture capitalist is going to look at the value of your company.

Question: At what point does a businessperson need the help of an investment banker?

Lynda: Usually when they're starting to think about raising outside money or selling their company.

Question: And how do you suggest that people seek out an investment banker? What's the best avenue?

Lynda: Usually people look for advice from other people who have raised money. We are frequently referred.

Question: What mistakes do you see women make during this process?

Lynda: I have been shocked by the number of successful businesswomen who will still sometimes say, "I have to talk to my husband about this." . . . I worked with one CEO and I kept telling her you can't say that, just say you need time to think about it.

Question: What must a CEO be able to talk about?

Lynda: You have to talk about the scalability of your company—how are you going to get the revenue growth? What are the leverages in your business where you can gain profitability? Not leverage like loans, but leverage in your operating business. They should also be able to talk about things like gross margin and EBITDA (see Chapter 6). A lot of people don't know the term *EBITDA*; they think my cash flow, my cash flow. But you can get a lot of

> mid-size company CEOs, men and women, who run
> profitable businesses but don't really look at their
> balance sheet and where their leverage is growing.

PINPOINTING VCs

Just like the process for finding angels, often the best way to start is locally—through business contacts and other networks. For instance, we asked our local banker and one of our micro lenders for recommendations. Both provided several potential investors and allowed us to use their name as a referral. In a world where VCs are besieged with unsolicited business plans, a recommendation carries substantial weight.

Beyond personal referrals, the Internet can also be a valuable tool to search for VCs in your specific industry. There are hundreds of them. There are also a number of Web sites offering centralized directories with VC groups seeking "deal flow," which is their way of describing prospective companies to invest in. See www.mominventors.com/millionairemoms for a list of venture capitalists.

CONCLUSION

As an entrepreneur you will need to call upon your own passion and belief in what you are doing to get to the next level, especially when you begin seeking money from outside sources. Remember that money is a tool to get you where you need to go. And know that others, especially nonentrepreneurs, won't always understand the challenges or recognize the logic, much less the sanity, of what you are doing.

Finally, overcome your own personal fears.

"Saying 'I don't have the money' is not an answer to anything," said Nell Merlino of Count Me In. "It's not a good enough answer."

The money is there . . . now go get it!

In the next chapter, you'll find strategies for how to juggle all your newfound responsibilities—managing your business while still managing your home, family, and children.

The Extreme Sport: Juggling Family and Business

Most women who work at any job outside the home face the challenge of finding balance in their lives: the right mix of work, family, and self. Becoming an entrepreneur, however, can heighten this challenge, because the scale can suddenly and without warning tip heavily toward business. The myth of entrepreneurship is that it affords more time for outside interests; the truth is that most business owners spend more time working—albeit on their own hours and their own terms—than they had with traditional nine-to-five jobs. For some, that can make balance easier; for others, more difficult.

Then there are those lingering societal expectations of what's "right" versus what's "wrong." You can always find someone who'll argue the merits of every extreme—from staying at home full time with the kids to the benefits of being a working mother. That's an argument that's not going away anytime soon. Add entrepreneurship to the mix and the complexity becomes intensified.

In this chapter, we'll examine the challenges of finding balance between entrepreneurship and family, and we'll learn how our Millionaire Moms faced and overcame these challenges. Some are still striving to find that balance as their businesses change and evolve, while others have found their groove and stuck with it. They all, however, share the ongoing struggle to manage all of it well. We'll also examine how these women took on, ignored, or dealt with lingering social pressures and expectations from outside "forces" like friends, extended family, other moms, and the media.

A DAY IN THE LIFE

If you are already running your business from home, the following story probably sounds very familiar to you:

At 4:00 a.m. my alarm went off for another accelerated business trip. As a mother of 3- and 5-year-old girls, I do my best to cram all travel meetings into the shortest period of time. This trip is no exception.

I make a much-needed pot of coffee and pull out a piece of construction paper and bright purple marker from my daughters' art kit. I draw hearts all over the page and tell the girls that I love them, hoping this little note will ease their concern when they wake up to find mom's gone on another business trip.

I head out to the airport, park the car, and leap onto the shuttle bus to the terminal. Among the sleepy-eyed travelers, I see a family with two little girls the same age as mine heading off for a family trip. I must fight back my tears. I then realize all the contradictions present in my life at that very moment—the sight of this family making me long for my own, a business book in my bag promising to teach me how to make millions, and a Dalai Lama CD in my player chanting about health (something I'd brought on the last three trips and still hadn't played).

After a frantic and exhilarating day of back-to-back meetings in New York with ABC's *Good Morning America*, Count Me In, and The

Center for Women's Business Research, I dash back to the airport, returning to California from my one night turn-around. I am determined to pick up my 5-year-old from preschool. There were no delays at the airport and I arrive at school on time—and am thrilled to see my daughter's radiant expression when I surprise her. The teacher promptly comes up to me and says, "You didn't turn in the form for the field trip and it was due two days ago and Sophia's library book is overdue so she wasn't allowed to check out a new book today." Standing next to me, a nonworking mom overhears this and comments, completely seriously, "You are such a bad mom." I am speechless. On some level I feel that she is right, even though rationally I am completely comfortable with my role. I walk back to my car in the preschool parking lot and burst into tears. I call my mom to share the story, and she told me to go punch that mom in the nose.

This slice from my own life illustrates so many of today's issues for women—guilt, career pressure, conflicted desires, outside judgment, and criticism. The pressure to do what's "right" comes from so many sources, it's often difficult to know what to do at any given moment. Satisfy the boss by working late or see your daughter's soccer game? Make time for a media appearance or make it to a friend's wedding? Clean the house or play with the kids? The choices can be overwhelming.

ACHIEVING THAT "PERFECT" LIFE BALANCE

There are those who've attempted to make a science of determining the proper life balance. In her article, *Yin and Yang: The Secrets Behind Achieving a Balance Between Work and Home*, writer Elizabeth Inskip-Paulk says, "Imagine your life as a pie chart, cut into eight equal pieces—this is what a balanced life *should* look and feel like."

This diagram depicts an optimal mix of eight aspects of life: Job/Business, Family, Friends, Leisure, Health, Personal Growth, Education, and Spirituality. This generally accepted ideal for achieving balance is a sincere attempt to help. But, alas, ideals tend to be

The Perfect Life According to Paulk's Model

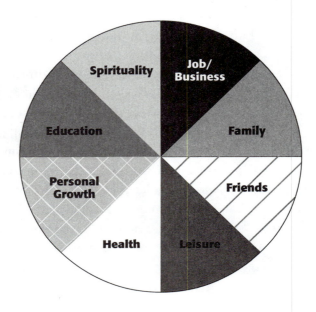

"noble lies." Pie charts may set a stage but they are not an indicator of joy, sorrow, and the other realities such as the plethora of activities that each of us face as part of our daily lives.

Therefore, rather than replicate the pie chart model, I created another model to help figure out what was real, and the results surprised me. This "day in the life" timeline breaks down my typical day. The key word here is "typical." This doesn't include sick kids, travel, conferences, trade shows, media events, and special projects—like writing this book. However, it suited my purposes to get a general idea of how my actual day looks. I should clarify that this exercise is not intended to create sympathy, admiration, or to focus on "me." It is solely intended to illustrate a point—we all have more to manage than can reasonably be parceled into equal slices of a pie chart.

Day in the Life of . . . Timeline

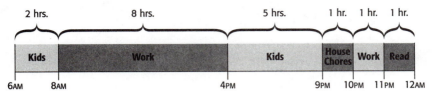

I discovered that I spend nine hours a day working, seven hours with my kids, one hour cleaning the house (dishes, laundry, and putting toys away), and one hour reading a novel before bed—that is if I can keep my eyes open for my one hour of "me" time. Finally comes six hours designated for sleep—whether that occurs or not. Children are not on the same schedule as entrepreneurial parents! Ours still wake up during the wee hours of the night. Recently, I was up until midnight rehearsing a speech that I was to give the next morning to a group of city officials in my area. One daughter woke up at 2:30 a.m. unable to fall asleep until 3:30 a.m., and the other woke up at 5:30 a.m. to start her day. What choice did I have but to perform as I was expected to?

Lastly, I made an additional list of all the "other" things that I feel obligated to do—what I call the "pulls" in my life.

1. Spend time with extended family. This is especially a struggle when there is love between family members, who want more time than the entrepreneur can manage.
2. Grocery shopping
3. Gas in the car
4. Laundry (loads and loads of laundry!)
5. Buy kids' clothes (I just noticed that one of my daughter's pajama bottoms was looking more like shorts rather than long johns.)

6. My kids' school projects (I feel stress when Sophia comes home with a week-long journal assignment that requires intense parental participation.)
7. Play dates
8. Household repairs/maintenance
9. Organize baby photos—create baby books
10. Organize closets and kids' play area and bookshelves
11. Community events (speaking invitations at conferences)
12. Thank-you cards and gifts (finding, shopping, writing, mailing)
13. Dry cleaning
14. Birthday parties (shopping for gifts, cards, wrapping)
15. Spouse (tending to marriage, dates, intimacy, fun)
16. Aging parents (wish to be with them yet feeling pulled in every other direction). I often wonder what my guilt quotient will be when they die. They reassure me that they are getting everything that they want from me, my husband, and children, but I still wonder.
17. Cooking meals (This is a stress for me because of all the other time constraints. Plus, with two preschoolers, you can work to make a nice meal and then they won't eat it anyway.)
18. Holiday planning (conflict between what I want and creating traditions for the kids)
19. Personal shopping (clothes, makeup)
20. Hair
21. Nails
22. Stack of unread business-related books next to my bed
23. Kids' haircuts, doctors' visits, school registration, and medical forms
24. Yard maintenance/gardening
25. Watering indoor plants
26. Keeping in touch with friends

If each item averaged just one hour per week (some would be longer and some would be shorter), this would add 26 hours of obligations (three full additional workdays) each week. Time, of course, that many of us do not have.

EXERCISE

Take a few minutes to both sketch your own "Day in the Life" timeline as well as create a list of your "life pulls." This may help bring clarity as to why you may be feeling overwhelmed, frustrated, or exhausted when you see your ever-mounting "to do" list. Seeing "what's real" about your life is the only way to recognize that the expectation of "balance" is a myth that exacerbates the pressure on an already over-stressed system. That said, this method also allows one to see more readily what items and obligations can be sacrificed or postponed.

When Julie Clark began Baby Einstein, she quickly learned what "doing it all" actually meant. "There were three things that were taking me in different directions," Julie says. "One was being a mom and a wife, one was the business, and the third was managing everything else—cleaning the house, doing the laundry, making personal appointments, going to the cleaners, and more. I looked at these three things and said, okay, which one don't I want to do—because I can't do all three."

This is an important point; some "necessary" tasks will never be done without help. As a driven entrepreneur, it may be that many of these tasks go undone for long periods of time—the reality of putting all of your energy and attention into creating something big.

It's this layer of pressure—the idea that one should strive for "Superwoman" status as measured by common cultural ideals—that exacerbates feelings of inadequacy and guilt, which I cover in the next section.

MILLION-DOLLAR SECRET

Jeanne Bice, who is 68 at the time of this writing, observes the reality of today's world. "Young women today think they have to be superwoman," said Bice. She compares it to when she was a young wife and mother in the 1950s and 1960s. "We are putting unreasonable demands on people. We did not go out to dinner every night. When we had parties, we did not have to be the entertainer—everyone brought a dish. That's the difference. Look at how you can make it work. Anything can work."

THE GUILT FACTOR

One mom I know (now a grandmother) recently confided to me that when her kids were growing up, she did everything "perfectly." Her hair and matching clothes were impeccable at all times. The kids were groomed, the house was clean, meals were made, social events were planned and came off without a hitch, photo albums were in order, holidays/major events were planned in advance . . . the list goes on. She was so worried about what others thought that she actually folded all of the kids' clothing inside their drawers before guests would arrive at her home.

Today, though, she recognizes the fallout of meeting all these societal expectations: she missed developing herself and her own interests. She also realizes that time spent focusing on the outside appearances (with her kids in the playpen while she ran around doing household chores) would have been better spent engaging with them.

Women have always been subject to societal expectations. "Super Mom" should have a perfect household, perfect marriage, perfect kids, and do everything with a smile on her face. In my experience, men don't generally seek the answer to the question, "How do I create balance in my life?" the same way women do. This makes sense—the predominant social expectation still pressuring men is to be a career star and make money. However, as women move more and more into the business realm, they are still expected to own the family obligations as well.

WHAT'S REAL?

The prevalence of conferences, articles, blogs, books, and every other form of discussion around balance illustrates the struggle women are having. The issue is real.

A recent QuickPoll conducted by CareerWomen.com™ revealed that the majority of women today are working 40 to 50 hours per week, and 53 percent of them are struggling to achieve work/life balance.

Scott Reeves, in an article for Forbes.com, points out that these women are still working just as much at home—which equates to two "full-time jobs!"

"The need for a varied work schedule affects both men and women, but caring for the children still falls heavily on the mother," Reeves explains. "Nearly half of the workforce is now female and about 85 percent of working women are, or will become, working mothers."

Even Madonna, with hundreds of millions of dollars and an army of servants at her disposal, has trouble achieving balance. In an interview with CNN's Larry King she was asked how she manages her life—balancing all of her roles: a marketer, a singer, an actress, a mother, a wife, and more. Madonna's response? "I live a highly scheduled life. There's absolutely no wasted time. I'm very focused and have a great assistant."

And of course not everyone has the staff Madonna has. In that same interview, King asked her what she thought people did without help and she replied, "When my nannies [note: plural] have days off, I ask the same question. How do people do this all the time? Taking care of children is a full-time job and I have total respect for women who do it completely on their own." (Excerpt from transcript: October 19, 2002).

Other Millionaire Moms believe that as you mature, other areas of your life can cause you to have a conflict of priorities. "When you're young, you really want to succeed in business and you want to make a big splash," says Karen Belasco. "But then you kind of grow into your life, and you realize a lot of things are very important, or should be more important, to you. I think, as a woman, that's where the difficulties come in."

Meanwhile, says Scott Reeves in Forbes.com, "Kids change everything." Whereas at one point in their lives, before having children, people could focus strictly on career, "an upcoming ballet recital or baseball game suddenly becomes more important than putting in crushing hours to nail the next promotion. You want to stay active in your field—and need the money—but you seek what eludes so many of us: a balance between work and home."

To me, balance is not measured on an equal scale in terms of time or cost—but instead is measured by whether you are doing what you feel is right for you. For example, many people become entrepreneurs out of dissatisfaction with their jobs. However, entrepreneurship does not automatically equal balance in terms of work versus the rest of your life. In fact, it can be the opposite if measured merely in terms of hours spent working. You'll probably work more hours. But your schedule may be more flexible or you may get energy in doing what you are passionate about, which may provide for greater balance.

The notion of "balance" is also a moving target—a process of constant questioning and adjusting that's more complex than diagnosing inequities in a pie chart. In other words, your idea of balance at age 29 will probably be changed by the time you're 39 and 49 . . . and you'll need to evaluate your priorities as you move through life.

Finally, remember that one person's idea of balance does not necessarily reflect yours. From a very early age, my parents told me that "comparison is the killer." To try to hold ourselves in comparison to others—or an unattainable ideal—means that we end up expending energy in a nonproductive way, and degrading our own self-esteem in the process. Whereas you may absolutely need one hour per day to exercise, I may need that hour to lose myself in a book.

That's why comparison to others and social expectations—like ideas of "perfection"—are detrimental to achieving satisfaction. Guilt and associated pressure are absolutely counter-productive. You are where you are.

Of course, that doesn't solve the problem. Even if you shut off the background chatter of unreasonable expectations established by others, there are still "pulls" that are entirely internal, natural, and positive—the pull to spend time with family, for instance, balanced with the pull to achieve success in your business.

CREATING YOUR OWN BALANCE

So where does that leave us? First, we must create our own definition of *balance*.

That's something that most of the Millionaire Moms did, either consciously or unconsciously. They certainly did not subscribe to many of the "standard" social expectations. They created their own set of requirements, and in most cases didn't allow negative self-judgments to stick to them.

The women interviewed in this book took specific steps to achieve balance, approaching the issue as a problem to be solved. While each had her own set of personal circumstances—whether it be divorce, a disabled child, caring for elderly parents, or a spouse's death—they each took on the challenge to achieve a balance that would work for them. And as I mentioned earlier, that balance can also change over time. Besides, the concept of balance may be a myth. All we can truly do is accept its ebb and flow which varies from moment to moment, day to day, and month to month. The reality is that there will be periods when the emphasis must go to the business and other times when the focus will be on the family. This requires the ability to adjust and adapt in the best way possible without adding feelings of guilt or self-criticism to the mix.

For instance, when Karen Belasco's kids were preschool age, they were with her at work every day. But now that they're a little older and she's not with them as much, she's facing a crossroads.

"I'm at a point in my life where I really want to focus on my family," Karen explained. "It's not because society is telling me that I shouldn't be working—that I should only be a mom—but more because my children are telling me 'Mom, we really need you.'"

Each mom approached various issues in different ways. The commonality they all share, however, is that there is no one solution or standard for all of them—and they all used their creativity to create rich lives that mix successful entrepreneurship and motherhood.

WHO'S THE BOSS?

Although almost every one of our entrepreneurial moms reported working more hours than they would in a "normal" 9 to 5 job, they also explain how running their own business creates entirely different possibilities.

Tomima Edmark explains the benefits of working for oneself. "There's a lot of license with being the owner," says Tomima. "I run the show."

Every day after school, Tomima's children come to her workplace—sometimes her home office, sometimes her off-site office. She talks about the luxury of being the boss, even if she's in a meeting with employees.

"My children walk in, the meeting stops, I give them a kiss, I talk to them." Tomima explains. "If I was the person sitting there with a boss, and my kids walked in, it would be a different animal."

By being in charge, Debi Davis also had the power to create a work environment tailored to her family's needs. "With any business I've ever had I always had a 'kid room,'" says Debi. "[The kids] were always welcome to be there and they could always interrupt me."

The benefits extended to her employees, as well. "It wasn't one-sided," Debi explained. "If somebody's kids were sick, you bring them to work, and we had a place they could be."

Kathy Gendel also talks about the freedoms that entrepreneurship provides. "A home office is great from the standpoint that you can pretty much call your own shots regarding timing, juggling schedules, that kind of thing," says Kathy. "You are your own boss and you are who you report to."

Julie Clark explains the benefits of "being the boss" in her own life. "I don't have more time, but I do have, in some ways, more freedom to do things that I love to do," says Julie. Her new business, The Safe Side, is structured in a way that allows her and her family to travel frequently—something they love to do. They are even planning to take a year off to travel around the world—an opportunity, Julie says, they would have never been able to take advantage of before the success of their businesses.

GETTING CREATIVE

Other women discussed how they simply created options for themselves.

"I traveled with my daughters many times," said Maria Sobrino who is a single mom. "I hired housekeepers at hotels to take care of them while I worked. As a mom, you're more comfortable working as long as your kids are just on the third floor, and not three or four hours away."

Once she could afford it, Julie Clark said she hired a part-time person to handle the "managing everything else" portion of her triumvirate list of responsibilities—the laundry, housework, and personal chores she just didn't have time to fulfill.

Madelyn Alfano, who is in the notoriously time-intensive restaurant industry, created a schedule that worked for her when her first son was born, rather than thinking she had to do things a certain way.

"I'd go to open the restaurant in the morning, come home in the afternoon, play with Max and have bath time," Madelyn says. She'd then go back to work at 6:30, right before Max's bedtime, and work at the restaurant until closing. This allowed her both to manage the business and spend time with Max.

Rachel Ashwell also created a schedule that gave her the work/home balance she needed. She made it a point to drop off her kids and pick them up at school, every day. She also hired trusted nannies to help out when she was working.

Because hers is an Internet-based business, Teri Gault takes advantage of the freedom to work from just about anywhere. Her family just bought an RV, which has allowed her occasionally to get creative with her workday.

"We'll go out to the lake and go boating, and I'll sit in the RV for part of the day and do e-mail, talk on the phone, do pricing reviews, maybe even a radio interview," Teri explained. She also made an executive decision to postpone temporarily her many media appearances, to make time for her son's impending wedding.

THE INSIDE STORY

Kathy Gendel

More than 10 years ago, Kathy Gendel launched her line of Breezies® Intimates, a wide range of undergarments sold exclusively on QVC (www.qvc.com). She and her husband, Craig, were running the business together, driving 180 miles each way to the QVC studio in the wee hours of the morning and late at night, so they could be home during the day for their three young girls. They've since moved closer to the studio to help create more balance in their lives.

In most ways, though, balance hasn't been a huge issue for them—in fact, their business and family lives are so intertwined, it's difficult to pinpoint where one begins and the other ends. Both have always been a group effort.

"The kids, at young ages, knew style numbers," said Kathy. "Instead of referring to this bra or that bra, they'd be quoting style numbers back to me." Today two of their three girls have joined the business, and now have their own product lines.

Growing the Breezies® business has truly been a labor of love. Kathy and Craig started the business using their unique talents—he was a panty manufacturer and she was a fashion merchandiser. They patented the fabric used in the panties and bra linings and the rest is history. Today theirs is a multi-million dollar business and a favorite on QVC.

Although they've worked hard, Kathy talks about the benefits of entrepreneurship, especially the example she's set for her daughters.

"I think they realize that women today really have no boundaries. They can be a mom; they can be in a business," said Kathy. "I think the girls, at a very young age, gained a true respect for their mother."

She also talks about what it's like working with your spouse. "You have to love to be with your partner or it just isn't going to work," Kathy said. "We're together 23 hours a day (he works out for an hour a day). And that's why it's been so successful. We're just a good team."

What motivates Kathy to keep creating, growing, and working?

"I would sure hate going back to corporate America. That's what drives me."

© Photo credit: Delka Ltd.

OUTSIDE SUPPORT

Realizing that at times it "takes a village"—that one person simply cannot do everything—has also helped some of our mom entrepreneurs.

When Max, Madelyn Alfano's son, was diagnosed with a disability, friends and family came to her aid to work with him when she couldn't be there. She is still grateful for their help.

Teri Gault talks about how her husband is her wingman, especially when it comes to her busy travel schedule. "He is always there for me," says Teri. "Knowing he's going to take care of everything while I'm gone—you can't buy that with any amount of money."

And in our family, starting Mom Inventors, Inc. has allowed my husband and me truly to co-parent our girls. We are both fully engaged in the company and in our family—a team when it comes to managing both "sides" of our lives. This was part of our living dream that we have already fulfilled—to work and parent side by side.

"Life is a team effort," said Jeanne Bice. "We are not out here alone."

REFUSE TO GIVE IN TO "CRITICS"

Another common thread among the Millionaire Moms is the confidence they have in what they are doing—and their refusal to give in to unreasonable criticism, expectations of how "femininity" should manifest, or misplaced guilt.

"I'm 68 years old now. I've worked my whole married life," said Jeanne Bice. "You make a choice on how to run your life. If you want to get caught up in the guilt, then be my guest and get caught up in the guilt . . . it's your choice to take it on."

She said she made a decision at one point to use the "big mouth" that God gave her and not hold back.

"I spent my whole life trying to be a sweet little wussy of a woman . . . and I'm a big-mouth broad!" said Jeanne. "It's very difficult for women because we've been told to be seen and not heard. A man can be pushy as all get-out, but if a woman is like that, she's bitchy."

I, personally, recall a situation when I was being interviewed about my first book on a local news show in Chicago. After the interview, when we were off camera, the male newscaster who had just interviewed me asked, point-blank, "Shouldn't you be home with your children?" I explained that they were home with their dad, a concept that seemed to confound him—even in today's "enlightened" society.

By defining your own lifestyle and creating your own requirements, you'll inevitably have to don your Teflon shield—no matter what you do or how well you manage, there will undoubtedly be critics from time to time. If you are confident in what you are doing—and that your efforts will ultimately benefit your children, yourself, and your family—it is easier to shove off the naysayers.

CREATE TIME FOR YOURSELF

The pattern among our business moms also reveals that after the business, the family, the kids, and the household, they tend to put themselves last. Even an occasional self-indulgence can send some into a tailspin.

"If I go get a pedicure once a month, I feel decadent and guilty," said Julie Clark. "The whole time I'm thinking, 'I'm a bad mom, I should be [with the kids].'"

Karen Belasco said that although running her own business gives her flexibility, she still feels the responsibility of the company at all times, which has prevented her from doing things like taking off on a vacation to France or an RV trip across the country.

"I would just find it so difficult to find the time to get away," Karen said.

But others have made it a point to find time for self-nurturing, like Teri Gault, who meets with a personal trainer two mornings per week to deal with health issues and stress. But it was initially difficult for her to do that.

"I'm a people pleaser, and I think a lot of women are. And so when I make a decision that's good for me, a lot of times I just have to buckle down and say, 'this is what I'm doing,'" explains Teri. "I think that's crucial for a woman to survive in business—to take care of ourselves. We can run ourselves ragged. I've been there a few times, on the brink of destruction."

Jeanne Bice concurs, explaining the need to carve out some personal time.

"I took time to sit and have coffee with my girlfriends and we would vent to each other. You have to have someone to vent to," Jeanne said. "If you don't, you will explode."

WEIGH YOUR PRIORITIES

Another key to gaining balance is the understanding that occasionally you have to turn off the business, which can be especially difficult if you run it from home, or with your husband or other family members.

Julie Clark explains that tuning out the business used to be very difficult for her. When the phone is ringing and the computer's in the next room, business is always pulling you in another direction.

"You really need to say, 'Okay, I pick up the girls at school at 3:30 and that's it. I'm not working any more tonight,'" said Julie.

MILLION-DOLLAR SECRET

"There's a point in time when—quite honestly—those extra three or four hours that you've just taken away from your family are not going to make a heck of a lot of difference to your company," said Debi Davis. *"You really just have to know when to say no."*

And sometimes that can include more difficult conflicts. Julie tells of one occasion when she was invited to a critical marketing conference across the country, but the invitation came just days after she had been away on another lengthy business trip. Her husband wanted her to go, but she made up her mind that she simply wouldn't—she didn't want to leave her kids again so soon.

In the September 2006 edition of O Magazine, writer Suzy Welch shared a tool she says helped her manage just about every personal and professional quandary in her life—The Rule of 10-10-10. It works like this: whenever you're in a situation where there appears to be no solution that will make everyone happy, ask yourself three questions:

- What are the consequences of my decision in 10 minutes?
- In 10 months?
- And in 10 years?

Suzy has used the rule to make some of her most meaningful decisions—including her divorce—to smaller ones—like deciding between staying late at work to preserve her chances for a promotion versus keeping a promise to her kids to be home on time.

THE INSIDE STORY

Julie Clark

For Julie Clark, family and kids always come first. And although a lot of people talk that talk, Julie is especially diligent about walking her talk.

Although you may know her as the high-level businesswoman who founded the phenomenally successful Baby Einstein Company—and sold it to The Walt Disney Company for millions—she never intended to create a multi-million dollar business.

"My situation is different from a lot of women who go into business to support their family or become wealthy or become incredibly successful—which is all great and valid," Julie explains. "I had a completely different motive."

Of course, all those things happened anyway—she became wealthy, successful, and made enough to support the family—but she started off simply wanting to make videos that would make babies and kids happy.

And in the back of her mind, as the company took off, she always worried about how she'd balance it all.

"For me personally, being a mom is more important than being a businessperson," Julie said. "If I could only pick one, I'd always pick being a mom."

But by running her business from home and knowing when to turn it off, she's managed to do both.

Today, her new company, The Safe Side, once again combines both her instincts—business and mothering—into a venture devoted to helping keep kids safe. She's partnered with John Walsh, the host of TV's "America's Most Wanted" to create a Web site, videos, and other tools that educate kids and parents on how to stay out of harm's way. In less than one year, they've already done over a million dollars in sales (www.thesafeside.com).

She says you must dig deep and ask yourself what the repercussions of a particular decision will be in 10 minutes, in 10 months, or in 10 years, and the answer to your conflict will become clear.

"I firmly believe it's incorrect to expect to do everything at the same time," said Deann Murphy, who launched her business in the 1970s with two children in elementary school. "You can do everything in your life if you're lucky, but you can't have the same intensity for all parts and pieces at the same time."

I follow a similar pattern in my own life. Although my children and large extended family are by far my first priority in a general sense, there are nevertheless many times when I must choose a business obligation over family. I weigh the consequences of each possible decision as the conflict arises.

Madelyn Alfano talks about how she balances being a good mom with being a good businesswoman.

"People really need to prioritize their lives," says Madelyn. "It's a matter of choices and what's most important. I think that if I wasn't a mom, I would have 100 Maria's Italian Kitchens today." (She has 10.)

Turning off the business can also be critical to maintaining balance in a marriage, especially if you and your spouse run the business together.

"When you're in business with your husband, the bedroom does turn into the boardroom," said Kathy Gendel. "You are living that business 24/7."

Teri Gault says for that reason, her family makes it a rule to turn off business during dinner . . . unless there's something really exciting happening.

In my own experience, I've come across and compiled some additional strategies that have proved useful:

- Plan free time as you plan work time. Like Teri Gault does with her personal trainer, make an appointment that you refuse to break with yourself — even if it's for an hour at the mall alone or 30 minutes of knitting before bed.
- Avoid distractions when at work. Work "smart," not long.
- If you work at an outside office, try to work from home sometimes—it'll save you that 30 minutes or hour that you would have been commuting.
- Keep one calendar for everything in your life (family, school events, and business meetings) so that you don't double schedule.
- Remember that a cell phone, a BlackBerry® or TREO® wireless device, and e-mail can be turned off; and every once in a while, do it!
- When at home, turn off the television. Instead, spend time with kids talking and engaging in activities.

- Take your kids to work and get them involved in parts of the business. Many of the moms in this book share that they included their children in the business from an early age. "My son says he cut his teeth on fabric," says Jeanne Bice. "My children have worked in the business their whole life. It is a family business now."

  Kathy Gendel has had a similar experience. "I created a situation where I could bring my two biggest passions together—my daughters and my business." Her two daughters have grown up to join the company. "I'm looking at my girls differently now. They are women entrepreneurs themselves. And that's my biggest delight."

- Schedule time with your significant other. Although "date night" can be difficult—finding child care can be a challenge and fatigue can certainly be an issue—it's important to schedule time for just the two of you, even if it's a candlelit dinner for two at home once the kids are in bed, or a glass of wine shared alone in the backyard.

- Get your kids to help out at home. Not only will you teach them that each member can contribute to the family, but it also builds their self-esteem . . . even at a young age. Recently, my five-year-old helped unload the groceries, and my three-year-old put away the 24-pack of toilet paper—walking each roll, one-by-one, down the hall to the utility closet. They were so proud!

PUTTING YOUR PLAN INTO ACTION

The most important way to achieve balance is to examine what's truly important to you as an individual—and avoid subscribing to others' ideals. Then put those priorities into action. Will there be sacrifices? Absolutely! Choices need to be made since not everything can possibly get equal attention. Only you can choose what is important to you and what needs to be set aside for the time being.

"I take my son to school every morning and most times I pick him up," says Madelyn Alfano. "But I've never had to wish for that. I just made it happen."

To create your own set of rules, it is first essential to identify those that are currently in play. I love the question that Steve Jobs asks himself:

"For the past 33 years, I have looked in the mirror every morning and asked myself, 'If today were the last day of my life, would I want to do what I am about to do today?'" said Jobs. "And whenever the answer has been 'no' for too many days in a row, I know I need to change something."

After Steve Jobs was diagnosed with cancer, his doctor informed him that it was incurable and he should 'prepare to die.' "I lived with that diagnosis all day," recalled Steve during his speech. Later that night, however, his doctors discovered it was a rare form of pancreatic cancer that surgery could—and did—cure.

"This was the closest I've been to facing death, and I hope it's the closest I get for a few more decades," explained Steve. "Having lived through it, I can now say this to you with a bit more certainty than when death was a useful but purely intellectual concept: no one wants to die . . .

"Your time is limited, so don't waste it living someone else's life. Don't be trapped by dogma—which is living with the results of other people's thinking. Don't let the noise of others' opinions drown out your own inner voice. And most important, have the courage to follow your heart and intuition . . . Everything else is secondary."

I hope you find a balance that works for you, too, and that this chapter has given you permission to accept the fact that it's impossible to do everything perfectly at the same time—but that you can do the things that are most important to you.

In Chapter 6, we'll talk about how women can better manage two important aspects of their business—money and people.

Managing Your Assets: Money and People

Among the most vexing challenges for women entrepreneurs are managing two of their most critical assets: money and people.

In Chapter 4, I talked about how to get the money you need for your business. In this chapter, the money challenge is to know, understand, and manage "the numbers" once your business is already established—and forecast and plan for future growth. In this chapter I aim to demystify and explain some basic financial concepts while sharing the insights of other successful women.

More so than any of the others in this book, this chapter is not for the faint of heart. However, based on my own experience, I feel it's essential. Over and over again I hear that it is in the area of money management that women are at a disadvantage. While others can help you manage this aspect—a chief financial officer (CFO) or an accountant—you still need a working knowledge of the concepts and key language. While I have leaned heavily on those experts who helped me in drafting this chapter, I have done my best to use clear examples and language that can be understood by those not typically invited to an accountants' convention! And please believe me, if I can learn it, anyone can.

Hiring and managing personnel is another ongoing issue for many women entrepreneurs. It is often difficult to know when the time is right to begin delegating the tasks you've always handled yourself . . . and hire your first employees. Then, once you hire them, you need to figure out how best to manage them and maximize their value to the company. Here, too, I will share tips from my own experience and from the successful Millionaire Moms who each handled personnel issues in very different and unique ways.

First, though, let's talk money.

UNDERSTANDING FINANCIALS

In the following pages, you'll be presented with numerous key financial terms, along with simple examples to illustrate them. Rest easy— my intention is not to turn you into an accountant! In fact, some hard core financial types may cringe at the simplicity of my examples. Rather, I aim to provide a basic working knowledge of some of the essential financial terms and statements. Understanding financials can also help you see the bigger picture and plan for growth you may have otherwise assumed impossible.

"Money plays a big role in both fueling and thwarting vision, which I think is a key piece to business growth," explains Nell Merlino of Count Me In. "Once you can see that big picture, how you think about almost everything is scaleable."

For a while I avoided the subject of financial management entirely, until it dawned on me that it was something I could learn, and that it would help me be a better businessperson. Lillian Vernon couldn't have said it better when I shared my fears with her—"You just gotta get over it." She's right. This understanding has given me a fuller view of how to manage and plan for growth; it's given me a greater sense of control, and has helped me make smarter decisions on a day-to-day basis.

There are a few aspects to managing the financials. The first is understanding the numbers, including how to use and read profit and loss (P&L), balance sheet, and cash flow statements. The second is creating and following a sound financial plan. And the third is creating an accounting system that keeps you organized and up to date on current financial activity. In this chapter we'll talk about all of these.

FINANCIALS, DEFINED

Although Lane Nemeth didn't enter the business world with any knowledge of financial management—she had been a school teacher—she nevertheless knew it was important to gain a working knowledge. Despite difficulties reading and recording the numbers due to her dyslexia, she learned how. She took accounting classes and relentlessly queried key employees, like her controller, for explanations on how it all worked.

"I never felt that not knowing something was stupid," Lane said. "I always thought it was great that I could learn."

Kathy Gendel has an even simpler explanation of why she learned the numbers. "I learned because I didn't want the bank to own my house," she says.

Part of the key to being an entrepreneur is in knowing what you don't know—and learning as you go along. The advice applies to financials—once they are broken down and understood, they are not nearly so intimidating! Plus, by learning what they're about and understanding the lingo, you will be taken more seriously as a businessperson.

Before the fear of the unknown sets in, it helps to look at financial statements as tools used in your business. Like any tool, it is important to keep it clean for it to work properly.

Generally speaking, *financials* refer to three interrelated reports:

- **Income statement** (a.k.a. profit and loss, or P&L). The income statement is the measure of your performance over a period of time. In short, it lets you know whether you are making money, and where your dollars are going.
- **Balance sheet.** The balance sheet is a photograph of where you are at any point in time. It provides the cash balance, inven-

tory level, a projection of money to be received and paid out, and other useful management tools.

- **Cash flow statement.** The cash flow statement is a tool that lets you know "why." Some call it a statement of sources and application of funds. It matters a lot whether the money in your bank account came from sales or from borrowing.

To illustrate how these three reports define the financial status of your business, I'll use an example from my own childhood and probably from your childhood as well: a lemonade stand. Because financials are the same, at their root, whether you're selling lemonade or Lear jets, I thought a simplified overview using my very first business might be a good way of easing into things.

MILLION-DOLLAR SECRET

"You have to have tremendous respect for money," advises Debi Davis. "You really need to know where your money is, how it works, and where it goes."

P&L/INCOME STATEMENT

An income statement (P&L) is a report that shows your business's operating performance for a particular period of time. The time period can reflect a day, month, a business quarter, a year—whatever you specify. This statement also has rows that indicate:

1. Your various forms of revenue (from lemonade sales)
2. Your direct costs of the revenue (what you've spent on supplies, like lemons, sugar, production, and getting product to store or warehouse)
3. Your general and administrative expenses of running the business (personnel, permit fees, rent, equipment, insurance, and taxes)

Your P&L also includes your "gross profit" and "net profit." These are figures you will need later.

Below find a basic example of an income statement. It is based on the following sales and expenses: Say I sold 10 $1 cups of lemonade in July, as I only worked one day. So, my gross revenues are $10. It takes one pitcher full of lemonade to fulfill sales of 10 servings. My four cost items to create this pitcher total $2: lemons ($0.50), ice ($0.75), sugar ($0.25), and paper cups ($0.50). This $2 in cost is referred to as the "cost of goods sold." I also incur a marketing expense, as well ($3 for poster board, tape, etc, to create two signs).

My gross profit of $8 ($10 in sales less $2 of cost of goods sold) produces an operating profit of $5 ($8 gross profit less $3 for all other expenses such as marketing costs). From my operating profits I have to deduct taxes to arrive at my net profit. At a 15 percent tax rate, I owe $0.75 of income tax, resulting in a net profit of $4.25. So, the net profit equals the gross profit minus all expenses that apply generally to the business as a whole (beyond production of the product or service), such as rent, staff salaries and benefits, insurance, marketing activities, professional fees, advertising, loan fees, research and development, computer equipment and support, and taxes. If you've mentally checked out here, go back again and again until you understand. Be especially kind to yourself while you are learning this information.

[Note: Retained earnings, to be discussed in the next section, is the profit a company is able to accumulate over time; it's also sometimes referred to as accumulated earnings. This is a new business, so the $4.25 is both the total profit and the current retained earnings. As profits accumulate, the daily profit figure will be different than the retained earnings. Retained earnings is the sum of the profits/losses of the business reduced by dividends paid over time.]

From this model it is also easy to come up with three additional numbers that can illustrate your financial performance: your "gross margin," "operating margin," and "net margin." Knowing these percentages is critical because they illustrate whether your company is financially viable, and if so, to what degree it will produce a profit.

Income Statement for the period ending January 1, 2007

Revenue	$10.00
Cost of goods sold	−$2.00
GROSS PROFIT	**$8.00**
Operating Expenses	−$3.00
OPERATING	**.$5.00**
INCOME/PROFIT	
Income tax	−$0.75
NET INCOME/PROFIT	**$4.25**

First, gross margin: this is the amount of money received from selling a product or service, minus the direct cost of producing that product or service. (Note that this does *not* include any of the expenses that apply to the general operations [the overhead] of the company.) The gross margin is a number especially important to a new business, because it indicates the strength of your core business model. If the gross margin is insufficient to begin with, the business's scalability (ability to grow into a large, profitable company) is questionable.

Gross margin (in dollars) = Pricing − Production cost

Gross margins are usually discussed in business as percentages. For example, "We have a terrific gross margin of approximately 80 percent. . . ." To get this figure, divide your gross profit (often referred to as gross margin) by your revenue. In this example, it's $8/$10 = .80. Remember, when speaking in terms of percentages, move the decimal two places to the right (.80 → 80.0) to come up with the percentage, .80 = 80 percent. The lemonade stand produced an 80 percent gross margin!

The second key percentage to know is your operating profit margin often referred to as operating margin. Calculate your operating profit by taking the gross profit (above) and subtracting the operating expenses of the business ($8.00 − $3.00 = $5.00). In the simplistic example so far, we only have $3.00 for marketing. However, these are expenses that generally apply to the business as a whole (beyond production of the product or service), such as rent, staff salaries and benefits, insurance, marketing activities, professional fees, advertising, loan fees, research and development, and computer equipment and support.

To calculate your operating profit margin as a percentage, divide your operating profit by your total revenue ($5.00/$10.00 = .50 or 50%).

Third, is your net profit margin. Also known as the "bottom line" net profit is calculated by deducting taxes from the operating profit ($5.00 − .75 = 4.25). To calculate your net profit margin or net margin, divide your net profit by total revenue (4.25/10 = .425 or 42.5%).

[Note: As companies grow, net margins can increase just by growing sales, because expenses can be spread across more revenue. For example, if you hire a receptionist at $25,000 per year when your company is earning $100,000 per year, your net profits will be significantly reduced. However, as you grow to $500,000 in earnings, assuming you still only need one receptionist, that cost is spread over more revenue . . . which means your net profit will increase. This brings up the concept of fixed and variable costs. The costs of the lemons, sugar, ice, and cups are more or less variable with the number of cups sold (there are exceptions such as quantity discounts, but this is not relevant in this context).]

Fixed costs are rent, labor, insurance, advertising, and so forth. The higher the volume of sales, the lower the fixed cost per item sold.

When you refer to gross margin or gross profit, the cost accountant will also call it the contribution to overhead and profit. Fixed costs are overhead. What's left after paying for the fixed costs is profit.

This is why higher volume is generally a good thing. The more you can sell of a product, the lower the fixed costs per unit. This brings your costs down. A little later, we'll touch on marketing concepts. The gross profit and fixed costs will be vital in setting your marketing strategy.

MILLION-DOLLAR SECRET

"There are plenty of schools that will teach you some basic accounting skills or how to understand what profit and loss means," said Mary Micucci of Along Came Mary Productions. "At the beginning, a person should do that. Then things don't become so scary."

Just when you are starting to "get" these numbers, you'll encounter someone who speaks this financial language with ease and flair. He or she will throw in the term EBITDA (pronounced Ee-bit-duh). This is an acronym that stands for **E**arnings **B**efore **I**nterest, **T**axes, **D**epreciation, and **A**mortization. These four items (I, T, D, A) are additional expenses that are generally nonexistent for very small or new companies, but can grow as a company expands. EBITDA is a "pro-forma" (i.e., to serve as a model) measure of income that is generally used by bankers and investors to measure the core operating earnings and cash flow potential of a business. In this lemonade stand example, EBITDA is not of much use, because the business presently has no meaningful *amortization* (repayment of a loan by installments), *depreciation* (allocation of the cost of an asset usable for a long term over the useful life of the asset), or *interest* (money paid to an institution, such as a bank, for loans to the company from that institution). And if your business is new, don't get hung up on understanding it now. However, more complex businesses will eventually need to know their EBITDA.

If you were to compare two essentially identical businesses, you would want to place them on an equal footing. Interest, taxes, depreciation, and amortization are important in seeing the bottom line, but not in determining the profitability. So by comparing the two businesses' EBITDA, you can get a truer comparison of their fundamental value. For example, if Sally finances the business herself, but Susie borrows operating capital, Susie will pay interest and Sally will not. When an outsider wishes to compare the basic businesses to each other, he will want to compare "apples to apples." To do this, he can look at the businesses' basic performance before the financing, taxes, and other costs (which have nothing to do with the core business results) are taken into account. This is what is meant by EBITDA and why it can be a useful tool.

BALANCE SHEET

So, now that you understand the key terms associated with your P&L, it's time to learn about your balance sheet. This statement reports the amount of your assets, liabilities, and capital (equity) in the business at a given point in time.

The fundamental math of a balance sheet is: Assets = Liabilities + Equity.

Your balance sheet shows your assets in the business (cash, inventory, etc.) versus how they are funded—through debt, like accounts payable (money you owe someone) or through vendor credit, loans, shareholder investment, or retained earnings.

Before we go deeper into illustrating a balance sheet with our lemonade stand example, there are some definitions you need to know:

- **Current asset:** Asset in a business that can be converted to cash in one year or less. These include cash, inventory, accounts receivable, and prepaid expenses.
- **Fixed asset:** Tangible asset such as facility improvements, equipment, and land, which is intended for long-term use. (These won't be converted to cash within a normal year.)
- **Intangible asset:** Things that have value for your company, but that you cannot touch, such as your reputation, patents, and goodwill.
- **Current liabilities:** Obligations of the business due within one year. These include accounts payable to suppliers, accrued expenses and taxes, and the portion of long-term debt that is due in the next 12 months.
- **Long-term debt:** Obligations of the business that are not due for at least one year.
- **Stockholders' equity:** The amount invested by stockholders, plus the accumulated profit of the business. Includes retained earnings, paid-in capital, and stock.

Let's move on to our lemonade stand. A balance sheet is presented below. It reflects the results from the income statement (P&L) plus a few other numbers, such as how the business was funded and what assets were purchased to support the business.

Let's start with inventory. On my first day of business I bought some supplies in bulk to achieve lower costs. We will assume for our example that I bought what I project to be sales of 10 cups per day, for seven days' worth of nonperishable supplies such as cups ($0.50) and sugar ($0.25), at a total cost of $5.25 ($0.25 + $0.50 = $0.75 times 7 = $5.25). I also purchased one of my perishables (lemons at $0.50 and ice at $0.75 for a total of $1.25). I would record $6.50 ($5.25 + $1.25) for these purchases into the inventory account. I would then deduct the cost of goods sold from the inventory account each day based on the amount used [assuming you use an equal amount each day, you would deduct $2 each day, as discussed earlier (see line 2 on balance sheet below)].

My supplier of nonperishable items gives me credit terms for my purchases, with the $5.25 cost resulting in an accounts-payable to that vendor (line 4 below), to be paid in 30 days. My perishables vendor requires cash on delivery, so I must pay for those purchases ($1.25) right away in cash. I also negotiated credit terms from my supply vendor on the $3 marketing costs (line 4 below), which is recorded in accounts payable as well.

Next, taxes are due on my income (I pay them quarterly). As a result, I will record (or "accrue," in accounting lingo) the tax liability in an accrued taxes payable account on the balance sheet. Lastly, my profit (what is left after paying my liabilities in line 6 from my assets in line 3) is recorded in the retained earnings account in the equity section of the balance sheet (line 7 below).

BALANCE SHEET AS OF JANUARY 1, 2007

Assets

Current Assets

(1) Cash $8.75 ($1.25 of my original $10 was spent on perishable supplies)

(2) Inventory $4.50 ($6.50 of purchases from vendors less $2 cost of goods sold)

(3) Total assets $13.25

Liabilities

(4) Accounts payable $8.25 ($5.25 of supplies and $3 on marketing)

(5) Accrued taxes $0.75

(6) Total liabilities $9

Equity

(7) Retained earnings $4.25

(8) Total liabilities and equity $13.25 (Liabilities $9 + Equity $4.25 = Assets $13.25)

Note on taxes: If you sell to consumers, you must collect and remit sales taxes. You will have federal and state tax on your income. Although some states don't have income tax, some cities and school districts do. Check with your tax advisor.

CASH FLOW STATEMENT

The cash flow statement shows the impact of cash flowing from three sources: (1) operating activities, (2) financing activities (borrowing money, selling stock, and repaying debt to finance the business), and (3) investing activities (including purchasing equipment and other fixed assets that will benefit the business over the long term). Amounts shown in the cash flow statement show actual cash amounts used or generated in these three types of activities. This statement reflects the cash that flows into and out of a business, and may be most relevant for a new company.

The amounts are calculated using certain items from your P&L, and then by calculating the change in certain balance sheet accounts. The purpose of the statement is to reflect the sources and uses of cash.

In the operating section, sources of cash include decreases in current assets (accounts receivable, inventory) and increases in current liabilities (accounts payable and accrued expenses). This sounds very "accountantish!" Just remember, a cash flow statement is showing what cash is available to your business. "Accounts Receivable" means you have given something to a customer and they owe you money—a receivable—for it. That is cash you don't have yet. On the other hand, an "Accounts Payable" is a debt you owe someone. You have received the good or service but have not yet paid for it. Therefore, you still have the cash. Uses of cash include increases in current assets and decreases in current liabilities.

In the investing activities section, sources of cash include bank loans and sale of stock in the company to investors. Uses of cash include repayment of bank debt. In the financing section, uses of cash include purchase of equipment and fixed assets.

CASH FLOW STATEMENT FOR THE PERIOD
ENDING JANUARY 1, 2007

Cash flows from operating activities

Net income	$ 4.25 profit available

Changes in working capital

Inventory	($4.50) Parenthesis here means minus or negative. Cash was spent to create inventory
Accounts payable	$8.25 This is positive because a "payable" is money owed—not yet paid. In other words, it's cash you still have in your possession.
Accrued taxes	$0.75 Owed but not yet paid
Cash flow from operating activities	$8.75
Cash flow from investing activities	$0
Cash flow from financing activities	$0
Net change in cash	$8.75
Beginning cash	$0
Ending cash	$8.75 [total above: $4.25 + ($4.50) + $8.25 + $0.75 = $8.75]

In reviewing my financials after a successful first day, I'm feeling pretty good. My P&L shows that I generated a great net profit (42.5 percent of revenue!). My cash flow statement shows I generated $8.75 of cash. But my balance sheet shows me with debts of $9 (see the balance sheet example above, line 6)—more than my cash! All of a sudden, I'm feeling I went backward. Did I?

No. It's important to take a look at my equity . . . the business has a net worth of $4.25 (balance sheet above, line 7). What happened is that I invested in inventory—$4.50 (balance sheet above, line 2) to support the growth of the business. I funded that investment with credit from my vendors and Uncle Sam (balance sheet, lines 4 and 5), since he'll wait until the end of the quarter for his tax payment.

Tomorrow, I won't have to purchase cups or sugar—just $1.25 in cash for lemons and ice. I'll spend another $3 on marketing (purchase an advertisement in a local newsletter), purchased on credit. On $10 of revenue, I'll generate another $4.25 of net income, and $8.75 of cash ($10−$1.25 for lemons and ice). At the end of tomorrow, I'll have $17.50 in cash. My equity will be $8.75, inventory will decrease to $3.75 (as I used $0.75 of sugar and cups), and my liabilities will be $12.75 (yesterday's balance of $9, plus $3.75 of marketing and accrued taxes), which is comfortably less than my $17.50 cash balance (money in my bank account). Voilà, I have a profit. What a difference a day can make!

This example illustrates a key point in financial management: tracking and trending of historical results and forecasting. Since your operating, investing, and financing activities play out over a period of time, it's useful, as well as important, to track results and then examine them over time with "trend analyses." Forecasts are like trend analyses; they just look forward as opposed to backward at historical results. The numbers, then, will tell us a story about my lemonade business as it progresses.

BUSINESS PLANNING

Once you understand these financial basics, you'll be able to apply your knowledge to create a financial plan for the future. Your financial plan puts your overall business concept (developed in Chapter 2) into a financial model that makes sense. This plan will help you actually "see" how the company can grow, and better prepare for it. It offers a big-picture look of where things are going.

"Women keep the vision of their business small because they haven't let themselves really imagine what it could be . . . probably because they're not sure how to do it or they don't know where they'd get the money," explains Nell Merlino. "So they constrain themselves from the beginning."

Building a financial plan from the outset can help solve this problem and expand your possibilities. In its most basic form, your financial business plan will take the best information available, augment it with reasonable estimates and guesses, and put it into a usable format. This is done by filling in a blank income statement for each month, going forward for as many months as possible. You can download the electronic version at www.mominventors.com/millionairemoms.

There are a number of elements your financial plan should include. First, though, you'll need to figure out your start-up costs. These are costs you'll have when starting up the business that won't likely be ongoing as the business evolves and grows. Every business will have different start-up costs, but some typical ones include permits and business licenses, professional set-up fees such as bookkeeping and incorporation documentation, lease deposits and facility improvement fees, beginning inventory, operating supplies, computers, infrastructure and other equipment, training, franchise fees, memberships, and more.

In my lemonade stand example, start-up costs include: two plastic tables ($20 each), a good blender ($25), four pitchers ($5 each), utensils and containers ($15), decorations ($20), a large cooler ($30), and a computer and software programs to help me run the business ($1,000). Total equipment purchases are $1,150. In addition, I need a business license and insurance, which will cost me $200 and $300, respectively, for the year, payable in advance. I also need to purchase my first week's supply of lemons, sugar, ice, cups, etc. ($200) for a total of $1,850.

FORECASTING

Forecasting is the critical element of financial business planning that estimates what will happen to a business in the future. Forecasts can be made for tomorrow, next week, next month, the next 12 months, three to five years, and beyond.

"Forecasting is an art," says Lane Nemeth. "There is no science. Once you've been in business three or four years, you know what your trends are, you know what your growth is, and there's a science to it. But at the beginning, there's no crystal ball."

Before we get into forecasting, there are some key figures you'll need to understand.

Revenue

To estimate your revenues, there are three elements to consider: price, capacity, and sales.

- **Price.** To arrive at the optimal price of the product or service you will provide (e.g., the lemonade that I plan to sell), it is important to consider two things: (1) the cost of producing and delivering a serving of lemonade, and (2) the price at which the market will purchase that serving, that generates the maximum profit. Don't confuse profit with revenue. My revenues are the total sales of lemonade. My profit, defined broadly, is how much I make after expenses.

To illustrate, let's use a simple scenario: If the cost of a single serving of lemonade is $0.20 and I sell 10 cups at $1 each, my revenue is $10 (10 cups × $1 per cup), my cost is $2 ($0.20 per × 10 cups), and my gross profit is $8 ($10 in revenues – $2 in costs). Would I sell more lemonade if I lowered my price? Probably. However, if I lower the price I'll make less money on each sale. So, I'll have to make more sales in order to make a higher gross profit. I can create a spreadsheet or chart that will help me determine how many servings I would have to sell at any given price in order to do better than an $8 gross profit. For example, if I drop the sale price to $0.50 in order to attract more sales and revenue, I will need to sell 27 cups of lemonade to achieve a gross profit higher than $8. If I think that 27 sales is an attainable number—and I won't have to buy more fixed-cost items such as equipment, or hire people to help ramp up to 27 sales—then my change in price makes sense.

I could do the same calculation, assuming that instead of charging $1 or $0.50 I charged $10 a serving. I would only have to make two sales to exceed that $8 gross profit. But, is it reasonable to assume that I could make two sales at that very high price? Once the sales process starts, customers and market forces will take over, driving the price to the optimal point. If a customer is unwilling to pay at least as much as my fixed costs plus variable costs plus a reasonable return, then I may be in the wrong business.

- **Capacity.** Capacity is the level at which your product or service can be delivered. In the lemonade stand model, my maximum capacity is dictated by factors like the amount of space available to store lemons, ice, and finished product. For my initial launch, I'll plan for a fairly low capacity to minimize my necessary investment. I base it on what I have currently— a small amount of refrigeration, one cooler, two portable tables, one blender, and four pitchers. I will be the sole employee. So, with those factors in mind, I will assume that the most lemonade I could make and serve would be four 10-cup pitchers per hour. Since peak foot traffic time near my stand is 10 a.m. to 3 p.m., and I need to buy lemons and ice in the morning, I will assume I can sell for five hours, for a total potential maximum of 200 cups per day, Monday through Friday.
- **Sales.** There is a wide range of philosophical and technical definitions around the concept of sales. From a financial perspective, sales are the intersection between the potential number of cups that could be sold (called the "demand potential") combined with the degree of success at reaching the prospective customers (called "penetration"), that produces revenue/ income to the business.

To figure out demand potential in our example, I consider the following:

My lemonade stand will be located on a busy sidewalk near the beach where many shoppers and workers walk every day. I've surveyed the space and found that approximately 200 people pass by each hour (1,000 in a 5-hour day). Obviously there could be any number of variables to consider in studying my target market such as gender, age, financial status, weather, and preferences for coffee or soda over fresh lemonade, etc. But, for the purpose of illustrating the forecasting concept, we can see there are 5,000 potential sales from Monday through Friday (5 days × 1,000 people per day).

To operate at full capacity (200/day) and to maximize my profit, I will need to sell a cup of lemonade, on average, to one out of every five people who pass by. One out of five is 20 percent. So, 20 percent is the market penetration I will need to operate at full capacity. There are a few ways to determine whether my target is a realistic one. First, I can test it. Second, I can evaluate sales of other similar businesses in the area. Third, I can research to discover what other lemonade stands have done in similar areas. And fourth, I can use my intuition. (That's where Lane Nemeth's description of forecasting as "art" comes in.)

Normally sales forecasts are based on a combination of these elements. But, in some cases it is all intuition, especially when other useful measures are unavailable. This is where the market is helpful in steering your business. For instance, if I find that I could sell more than 1,000 cups per week—my current capacity—I can maximize my profit by selecting one of the following three approaches: (1) raise my price until the number of cups I sell drops to within my current capacity of 200/day, (2) invest in the business to expand my capacity to meet the demand at the current price, or (3) reduce the scope of my operation until my sales match my capacity (e.g., by reducing my hours of operation). A word of caution: if you create demand and don't adjust to meet it, competition will be eager to step in to satisfy this demand. Once they join in, they will not be content to sell just enough to meet your unfulfilled demand, but will seek to take your core market share as well.

Cost of Goods/Services

To create a workable forecast, you'll also need to figure out the cost of goods/services. To do this, add up the costs of the core elements necessary to deliver your product or service. In order to pour 200 cups in a day, 20 pitchers will have to be made because each pitcher will fill 10 cups (20 pitchers × 10 cups = 200 cups). How much does it cost to produce my lemonade in a day—lemons, water, ice, sugar, labor? If my costs are $2 per each 10-cup pitcher, they are $40 per day ($2 × 20 pitchers = $40).

Operating Costs

To determine the operating costs for my forecast, I will have to consider how much it costs to pay myself and run the operation. Operating costs include line items like wages, rent, utilities, marketing, plus the portion of my fixed assets and other start-up costs that I must amortize.

For our example, we'll say that rent will be $500 per month, based on my lease, or $16.67 per day. Marketing is budgeted at $300 per month, or $10 per day. Insurance and business licenses are $500 per year, or $1.39 per day. If I pay myself $10 per hour and figure in another $10 per day for all other unexpected expenditures, my operating costs are $119.19 per day. At a gross profit of $0.80 per cup (80 percent of $1 price), I need to sell 149 cups per day to break even. Here is how I determined this need: $119.19 ÷ $0.80 = $148.98 (rounded up to 149). You should always assign a fair wage to your efforts. Often, proprietors end up working for free because they didn't budget for owner's wages.

BENEFITS OF FORECASTING

Now it's time to put all this information together. To create a basic forecast, start with one week's worth of business. Once that is complete, it becomes easier to expand to monthly and then yearly forecasts. See Chart 6.1 for my final one-week forecast for the lemonade stand.

Note: Under revenue assumptions, the total labor hours per day includes five hours open for business, plus three hours for purchasing, setup, and cleanup. (To find the source of some of the other figures such as depreciation, marketing, and other cost assumptions see Assumptions in Chart 6.3.).

Your weekly forecast is an important management tool. You use it to estimate sales, which will determine your labor requirements as well as your supply purchases. It's also important to consider seasonality and other influences on sales when forecasting. Tracking and noting sales trends, over time, will be an invaluable source of data to help you forecast and run your business profitably as time goes on.

A good sales forecast is also critical to help you avoid purchasing too much (wasting supplies reduces gross margin, and unnecessarily burns cash), or purchasing too little (there's nothing worse in business than to run out of product with people in line waiting to buy). Your forecast can also determine factors you hadn't considered. In the lemonade stand example, for instance, I find I'll still incur expenses when closed on Saturday and Sunday. I will need to factor these costs into my pricing, as discussed previously, to ensure that when I set my prices these costs are covered.

Chart 6.1

Weekly Forecast

	Unit factor	Monday	Tuesday	Wednesday	Thursday	Friday	Saturday	Sunday	Week
Revenue assumptions									
# cups per hour		40	40	40	40	40	0	0	200
# hours open		5	5	5	5	5	0	0	25
# cups per day		200	200	200	200	200	-	-	1,000
# pitchers per day	10	20	20	20	20	20	0	0	100
Price per cup		$ 1.00	$ 1.00	$ 1.00	$ 1.00	$ 1.00	$ 1.00	$ 1.00	-
Total labor hours per day *	3.00	8	8	8	8	8	0	0	40
Revenue	$	$ 200.00	$ 200.00	$ 200.00	$ 200.00	$ 200.00	$ -	$ -	$1,000.00
Cost of Revenue									
Lemons	$ 0.50	10.00	10.00	10.00	10.00	10.00	-	-	50.50
Sugar	$ 0.25	5.00	5.00	5.00	5.00	5.00	-	-	25.25
Ice	$ 0.75	15.00	15.00	15.00	15.00	15.00	-	-	75.75
Lemonade costs	$ 1.50	30.00	30.00	30.00	30.00	30.00	-	-	151.50
Cups	$ 0.50	10.00	10.00	10.00	10.00	10.00	-	-	50.50
Total cost of goods	$ 2.00	40.00	40.00	40.00	40.00	40.00	-	-	202.00
Gross Profit		160.00	160.00	160.00	160.00	160.00	-	-	800.00
Gross Margin									80%
Operating expenses									
Labor	$ 10.00	80.00	80.00	80.00	80.00	80.00	-	-	400.00
Other operating	$ 10.00	10.00	10.00	10.00	10.00	10.00	-	-	50.00
Marketing	$ 10.00	10.00	10.00	10.00	10.00	10.00	10.00	10.00	70.00
Rent	$ 16.67	16.67	16.67	16.67	16.67	16.67	16.67	16.67	116.67
License & Insurance	$ 1.39	1.39	1.39	1.39	1.39	1.39	1.39	1.39	9.72
Depreciation	$ 1.13	1.13	1.13	1.13	1.13	1.13	1.13	1.13	7.94
Total operating exp		119.19	119.19	119.19	119.19	119.19	29.19	29.19	646.39
Operating income/profit		$ 40.81	$ 40.81	$ 40.81	$ 40.81	$ 40.81	$ (29.19)	$ (29.19)	$ 153.61
Operating margin									15.4%

*Includes 5 hours open, plus 3 hours for purchasing, set up, and clean up.

THE INSIDE STORY

Tomima Edmark

Tomima Edmark launched her entrepreneurial career by inventing TopsyTail, a hair accessory that became an overnight phenomenon and instant success, garnering more than $100 million in sales since its launch in 1991.

She currently serves as the president and founder for the Andra Group, the parent company to two successful Internet retail undergarment Web sites: www.herroom.com and www.hisroom.com.

Tomima has worked hard to create these successes. She received her MBA from the University of Texas, Austin in 1983 and was named outstanding MBA finalist. After that, while working full time in the corporate world, she brought her TopsyTail vision to light, working evenings and weekends to make it happen. She even wrote and sold a book to fund her first TopsyTail prototype.

"Ninety percent of your success is just showing up," Tomima advises women entrepreneurs. "Take it as far as you can and do something. Make your prototype. Do some research. Talk to people. I think that's really the difference. That's what sets successful people apart."

Building on the success of TopsyTail, she launched her Internet retail Web sites in 2000. In addition to running the company, she also provides an "Intimate Wisdom" blog on the Web sites, which discusses issues related to the best fit of the garment, style, trends, and more.

How do you know when you've "made it" in business?

"I guess when you hear somebody's name over the company intercom and you don't know who they are!" joked Tomima.

Tomima has two daughters, ages eight and ten.

At the inception of your business, a good, well-thought-out set of projections is important to outside parties such as financial lenders (bankers, investors) and vendors (who will be deciding whether to extend credit to you). You'll also greatly benefit from the knowledge gained just from the process of creating these projections.

WORKING WITH YOUR FORECAST

Your forecast is not set in stone. Once you develop your own, similar to the one in Chart 6.3, the next step will be to review, revise, and test your assumptions. Inevitably, questions and problems will surface.

WHAT'S IN A FORECAST?

Your forecast should help you answer key questions such as: How do I make money? How much money will be required to launch and operate this business? And, most importantly: What's in it for me?

Once again, I'll use my lemonade stand to demonstrate how to analyze my forecast.

Chart 6.2, 12-Month Forecast, extends my forecast out over 12 months. The resulting forecast shows that in theory, this is a healthy business. It also shows how much money will be needed to fund it.

Chart 6.2

12-Month Forecast

Income Statement	Unit factor*	Jan	Feb	Mar	April	May	June	July	Aug	Sep	Oct	Nov	Dec	Year
Revenue assumptions														
# cups per hour		40	40	40	40	40	40	40	40	40	40	40	40	40
# hours open/day		5	5	5	5	5	5	5	5	5	5	5	5	5
# cups per day		200	200	200	200	200	200	200	200	200	200	200	200	2,400
# pitchers per day	10	20	20	20	20	20	20	20	20	20	20	20	20	240
Price per cup		$1.00	$1.00	$1.00	$1.00	$1.00	$1.00	$1.00	$1.00	$1.00	$1.00	$1.00	$1.00	-
# days in month		31	28	31	30	31	30	31	31	30	31	30	31	365
# days closed		9	8	9	8	9	8	9	9	8	9	9	9	104
Number of days open		22	20	22	22	22	22	22	22	22	22	21	22	261
# cups sold per month		4,400	4,000	4,400	4,400	4,400	4,400	4,400	4,400	4,400	4,400	4,200	4,400	52,200
# pitchers sold per month		440	400	440	440	440	440	440	440	440	440	420	440	5,220
# hours labor per month	3.00	176	160	176	176	176	176	176	176	176	176	168	176	2,088
Revenue		$ 4,400	$ 4,000	$ 4,400	$ 4,400	$ 4,400	$ 4,400	$ 4,400	$ 4,400	$ 4,400	$ 4,400	$ 4,200	$ 4,400	$ 52,200
Cost of Revenue														
Lemons	$ 0.50	220	200	220	220	220	220	220	220	220	220	210	220	2,611
Sugar	0.25	110	100	110	110	110	110	110	110	110	110	105	110	1,305
Ice	0.75	330	300	330	330	330	330	330	330	330	330	315	330	3,916
Lemonade costs	1.50	660	600	660	660	660	660	660	660	660	660	630	660	7,832
Cups	0.50	220	200	220	220	220	220	220	220	220	220	210	220	2,611
Total cost of goods	$ 2.00	$ 880	$ 800	$ 880	$ 880	$ 880	$ 880	$ 880	$ 880	$ 880	$ 880	$ 840	$ 880	$ 10,442
Gross Profit		$ 3,520	$ 3,200	$ 3,520	$ 3,520	$ 3,520	$ 3,520	$ 3,520	$ 3,520	$ 3,520	$ 3,520	$ 3,360	$ 3,520	$ 41,760
Gross Margin		80.0%	80.0%	80.0%	80.0%	80.0%	80.0%	80.0%	80.0%	80.0%	80.0%	80.0%	80.0%	80.0%
Operating expenses														
Labor	$ 10.00	$ 1,760	$ 1,600	$ 1,760	$ 1,760	$ 1,760	$ 1,760	$ 1,760	$ 1,760	$ 1,760	$ 1,760	$ 1,680	$ 1,760	$ 20,880
Other operating	10.00	220	200	220	220	220	220	220	220	220	220	210	220	2,610
Marketing	300.00	300	300	300	300	300	300	300	300	300	300	300	300	3,600
Rent	500.00	500	500	500	500	500	500	500	500	500	500	500	500	6,000
License & Insurance	41.67	42	42	42	42	42	42	42	42	42	42	42	42	500
Depreciation	34.03	34	34	34	34	34	34	34	34	34	34	34	34	408
Total operating exp		$ 2,856	$ 2,676	$ 2,856	$ 2,856	$ 2,856	$ 2,856	$ 2,856	$ 2,856	$ 2,856	$ 2,856	$ 2,766	$ 2,856	$ 33,998
Operating income		$ 664	$ 524	$ 664	$ 664	$ 664	$ 664	$ 664	$ 664	$ 664	$ 664	$ 594	$ 664	$ 7,762
Operating margin		15.1%	13.1%	15.1%	15.1%	15.1%	15.1%	15.1%	15.1%	15.1%	15.1%	14.2%	15.1%	14.9%

*Unit factor is the heading for the column that reflects basic cost or unit numbers. These are used to reflect costs, revenues, or other figures in columns to the right.

◆ 164 ◆

Chart 6.2 (*Continued*)

		14	13	12	10	9	8	7	6	5	3	2	1	91
Interest expense	15%	14	13	12	10	9	8	7	6	5	3	2	1	91
Income taxes		98	98	98	98	98	98	99	99	99	99	89	99	1,151
Net income		$ 567	448	$ 566	566	$ 566	566	$ 566	566	$ 565	565	506	$ 565	$ 6,611
Net margin		12.9%	11.2%	12.9%	12.9%	12.9%	12.9%	12.9%	12.9%	12.8%	12.8%	12.0%	12.8%	12.7%
EBITDA		698	558	698	698	698	698	698	698	698	698	628	698	8,170

Balance Sheet

	Inception	Jan	Feb	Mar	April	May	June	July	Aug	Sep	Oct	Nov	Dec
Cash	-	835	1,286	1,896	2,224	2,825	3,425	3,731	4,331	4,932	5,236	5,761	6,367
Inventory	200	220	200	220	220	220	220	220	220	220	220	210	220
Prepaid expenses	500	458	417	375	333	292	250	208	167	125	83	42	(0)
Total current assets	700	1,514	1,903	2,491	2,778	3,337	3,895	4,159	4,718	5,277	5,539	6,013	6,587
Equipment	1,150	1,150	1,150	1,150	1,150	1,150	1,150	1,150	1,150	1,150	1,150	1,150	1,150
Accumulated depreciation	-	(34)	(68)	(102)	(136)	(170)	(204)	(238)	(272)	(306)	(340)	(374)	(408)
Net equipment	1,150	1,116	1,082	1,048	1,014	980	946	912	878	844	810	776	742
Total assets	1,850	2,630	2,984	3,539	3,792	4,316	4,841	5,071	5,596	6,121	6,349	6,789	7,328
Accounts payable	75	330	300	330	330	330	330	330	330	330	330	315	330
Accrued income taxes	-	98	174	272	98	196	295	99	197	296	99	188	287
Loan	1,675	1,535	1,396	1,256	1,117	977	838	698	558	419	279	140	-
Total liabilities	1,750	1,963	1,870	1,858	1,545	1,503	1,462	1,127	1,086	1,045	708	643	617
Retained earnings	-	567	1,014	1,581	2,147	2,713	3,279	3,845	4,410	4,976	5,541	6,046	6,611
Paid in capital	100	100	100	100	100	100	100	100	100	100	100	100	100
Total equity	100	667	1,114	1,681	2,247	2,813	3,379	3,945	4,510	5,076	5,641	6,146	6,711
Total liabilities and equity	1,850	2,630	2,984	3,539	3,792	4,316	4,841	5,071	5,596	6,121	6,349	6,789	7,328

Chart 6.3

Assumptions

Cost of Goods

	Per Pitcher	Weekly Volume	Per Week
Lemons	$ 0.50	100	$ 50.00
Sugar	0.25	100	25.00
Ice	0.75	100	75.00
Subtotal	1.50		150.00
Cups	0.50	100	50.00
Total cost of goods	$ 2.00		$ 200.00

Start-up Costs

		Total cost	Life	Cost/month	Cost/day
Equipment					
2 Tables	$ 40.00		24	$ 1.67	$ 0.06
Blender	$ 25.00		24	1.04	$ 0.03
4 Pitchers	$ 20.00		24	0.83	$ 0.03
Utensils & containers	$ 15.00		24	0.63	$ 0.02
Decorations	$ 20.00		24	0.83	$ 0.03
Cooler	$ 30.00		24	1.25	$ 0.04
Computer system	$ 1,000.00		36	27.78	$ 0.93
Fixed assets		$ 1,150.00		$ 34.03	$ 1.13
Business License	200.00		12	$ 16.67	$ 0.56
Business Insurance	300.00		12	25.00	$ 0.83
Prepaid expenses		$ 500.00		$ 41.67	$ 1.39

Inventory	1 week supply	
Paper cups	50.00	
Sugar	25.00	
Subtotal—on terms		75.00
Lemons	50.00	
Ice	75.00	
Subtotal—C.O.D.		125.00
Total inventory costs		$ 200.00
Total Start-up costs		$ 1,850.00

Other Operating costs
Fixed

Rent	$ 500.00	per month

Variable

Marketing	$ 300.00	per month
Other operating	$ 10.00	per day
Labor	$ 10.00	per hour

Total labor hours per day

Open hours	5.00	hours selling
Other	3.00	purchasing/setup/cleanup & close
Total	8.00	

Founders stock investment	100
Loan	1,675
Start-up inventory on terms	75
Total start-up investment	1,850
Interest rate on loan	10%
Loan repayment (months)	12
Loan repayment terms	24

MILLION-DOLLAR SECRET

"Sales hide a multitude of sins," said Madelyn Alfano. "When your sales are big, yes you have your profits, but you may not know if it's just due to the volume. If your item is not marked profitably enough, it's not going to last. So you have to constantly look at the numbers—sales numbers, cost of goods sold, and profits."

From the Income Statement on the 12-Month Forecast in Chart 6.2, I see that my hard work produces $52,200 of annual revenue (see line labeled Revenue), a salary of $20,880 (see line labeled Labor), and net profits of $6,611 (see line labeled Net income). From the balance sheet, I note that I need a start-up investment of $1,850 (see Balance Sheet first column, last line) to launch the business, which I will fund with $100 of my own money, a $1,675 loan, and $75 of vendor financing (accounts payable). Further, I maintain very comfortable levels of cash and debt. I see that I will generate $7,762 of operating income, and have $6,367 of cash left over (see Balance Sheet line labeled Cash).

This looks great to me! So I start showing these projections to a few friends and trusted advisors to get their input and make modifications as necessary.

AT-A-GLANCE MONEY MANAGEMENT SCHEDULE

Build regularly scheduled time into your week and month to review the numbers. If this means producing a set of reports the same day each week and month, put it into your calendar. If it means a regularly scheduled meeting with your financial advisor, this is a good idea as well. Here's a simple review schedule that works for me:

Frequency	Report/metric name	Looking for
Weekly	Accounts Receivables Aging	Money due to company, late customers who need a reminder
Weekly	Account balance	Available cash for bills and investment
Weekly	Accounts Payable Aging	Who needs to be paid, who we are spending a lot of money with
Monthly	Sales	Progress in sales, revenue generated, performance against forecast, inventory requirements. (Are we running low on any particular product?)
Quarterly	Gross margin	Gross margin percentage actually earned compared with what we had forecast in our plan. Are the sales and production prices in sync? Are transit costs under control?
Quarterly	Net margin	What is your net margin percentage compared with your forecasted net margin percentage? Determine if business is scaling. Are expenses in line with growth?
Yearly	Revenue, Gross and Net margins	Is business on plan? Multiples of transactions of similar businesses in our markets.

HELP FROM EXPERTS

While it's important to have a fundamental understanding of your company's financials, that doesn't mean you have to take on CFO duties on a day-to-day basis. In fact, as your company grows and you begin delegating and hiring personnel, a trusted financial expert can be your best ally.

Many of the women I interviewed count on a financial consultant, accountant, or CFO.

BANK ON THIS

Lynda Davey, an investment banker who's helped many entrepreneurial businesses find venture capital funding, says it's not a negative if an entrepreneur—male or female—counts on a skilled financial person as long as they know and understand the key numbers.

"You can't fake it, but if you know which ones are important then you make a very good team with your CFO," explained Lynda. "A lot of small entrepreneurs don't understand the importance of 'the numbers.'"

PERSONNEL MANAGEMENT

Just as your financial person will become a key contributor to your business, you'll eventually reach a point where you'll have to hire additional personnel. Most business owners agree that employees can make a big difference in their success.

"The most important thing is people," says Teri Gault of The Grocery Game. "When it comes down to it, it's the people who make it happen. The machines can't do it all."

Her employee retention rate speaks volumes—except for one employee, everyone she's hired since she launched the company is still with her.

But the hiring, managing, and firing of employees can also be a daunting task—especially for women, who have a greater tendency to get more personally involved with their employees rather than viewing them objectively as a business resource. In some cases, it can hurt the business to blur the lines between business and personal concerns.

When Madelyn Alfano hired a consultant a number of years ago to help evaluate her business, for instance, he told her she needed to stop mothering her employees so much.

"He said I had to expect as much from my employees as I expect from myself," says Madelyn. "I needed to create a new threshold of tolerance for quality in staff. That was a very good lesson."

Terrie Williams approaches staff management with a similar blend of sensitivity and firmness. "I had 15 employees at one time. I have a very boutique-size organization now, and when I have projects that I want to take on, I subcontract out. If I see that somebody is off his or her game I will address it, give them some time to talk about it, and then it's 'we have work to do.' No ifs, ands, or buts. I am demanding—but fair. And I honor the fact that people are wounded. We still have got to get this job done and I have every expectation of that, but I'm also going to give the process its time."

Karen Belasco had similar difficulties when it came to staffing issues. When she first started, she had her husband fire employees when it became necessary. "When I'm talking to them one day and asking about their family—knowing that they're really not cutting it—I couldn't turn to them and say 'you're fired,'" Karen explains. Although she now takes on this task herself, it's been a challenging process.

For Deann Murphy, staff management was one of the primary reasons she eventually decided to sell her company. "When you have a staff between 50 and 200, you have a lot of management issues," says Deann. "I determined that my very best skills were not being a corporate manager or chief operating officer. They were being on the creative side, the product development side, the sales side. So as these things became more evident, I said, 'Okay, I have choices here.'"

I believe it's a woman's innate sense of personal responsibility to her employees, though, that can also drive the business to achieve greater success.

When Maria Sobrino hit a low point in her business years ago, she considered getting out. "But then you start thinking—oh my God, if I close my doors, look how many people are going to be out of jobs," shares Maria. "Suddenly you can't stop."

Maxine Clark could have retired to a tropical beach with her earnings from years of hard work in the corporate world, but her sense of personal responsibility didn't allow it. "I didn't need to start this company," Maxine says. "It's really about personal accomplishment, making a difference, helping other people see their potential. Because other people helped *me* get to that level."

THE INSIDE STORY

Madelyn Alfano

Madelyn Alfano has applied smart, thoughtful management of both money and people to become one of California's most successful restaurant owners. She grew up in Hoboken, New Jersey, in a big Italian family who always worked in the food business.

In 1985, Madelyn opened her first Maria's Italian Kitchen in Sherman Oaks and named it after her mother. An immediate success, the concept was expanded to other locations throughout greater Los Angeles. There are now 10 Maria's Italian Kitchens, each of which offers healthy, quality food based on family recipes brought over from the old country.

Madelyn is often on the road from location to location, overseeing nearly 500 employees. She's always strived to create a supportive, comfortable culture at her restaurants. It's an extension of her warm, family-oriented personality.

Madelyn explains, "Whether you're an employee or a customer, I want you to feel as if you're part of a big, close-knit family that supports and cares about you."

This appears to be working as her company is considered one of the leading privately owned restaurant chains in the state. Madelyn is deeply involved with numerous charities and nonprofit organizations, including The Max Reitzin Memorial Fund, which Madelyn created in memory of her son, to benefit handicapped children.

She has another teenage son, Nicolas, who is a passionate entrepreneur and has embraced the philosophy of giving both in time and money to make a difference in this world.

Her inclination to give also extends to her employees and customers.

"I used to loan everybody money," said Madelyn. "I have 500 employees now, I can't do that. Certain policies I've become stricter on."

Nevertheless, her company remains a family-oriented place to work—a fact you immediately feel when you sit down at one of her restaurants for a delicious, home-cooked Italian meal (www.mariasitaliankitchen.com).

Madelyn reconnected with her junior high school friend, Dr. Jeffrey Tucker, married him in 2005, and feels blessed to have Jeff's children Josh and Danielle as part of her family.

© Photo credit: Terri Sutherland

There are other reasons that personnel issues present a unique challenge to women entrepreneurs. Because we have been faced with fitting our personal and family lives into our own careers, we are expected to be more understanding of staff's work/family conflicts.

And like Madelyn Alfano, many of us fall into a motherly role. After all, we are responsible for the work and performance of our employees. They depend on us for their money and we have the power to say "yes" or "no" in many things they do on a daily basis. It's no wonder the role of "boss" is so easily confused with that of "mom."

In an *Entrepreneur* magazine column by Aliza Pilar Sherman called "The Perks of a Woman-Owned Business," wellness lifestyle expert Terra Wellington says, "Women business owners must consider two things before implementing perks: First, don't lose sight of the fact that you aren't your employees' mother. Second, remember you are still running a business, first and foremost."

So, how do you find the people who will make a difference to your company, and who will reach their personal potential? There are a number of philosophies and approaches to hiring. Using the method that works for you is the most important. The key to all of them, though, is to know what you are looking for *before* you begin your search. These include pinpointing the most important traits you'd like in your new hire, including:

- Specific technical skills
- Experience and maturity level
- Interpersonal disposition

For example, if you're hiring a receptionist who also will be writing memos and doing data entry, your specific needs might be comfort with a keyboard, basic knowledge of Microsoft Windows programs, and an expressive and friendly personality.

You should also do some basic research about salary as it relates to work responsibilities. This information isn't difficult to find. First, speak to other business owners about similar roles in their companies. Second, visit job search Web sites and read want ads and resumes that relate to your position. Some sites where you can find this information are monster.com and careerbuilder.com. Salary.com also can give you good insights into what you can expect to pay them.

"The right person will save you more than a salary every time," says Lane Nemeth.

Once you narrow down your list of candidates, think through your list of questions before you start interviewing. This will give you more confidence when you interview and will help you gain greater insights into your candidates' attributes. Additionally, it will set a professional tone with your candidate from the first meeting. Keep in mind that you are not only looking to gain specific information from your questions but that you are also seeking to learn how your candidate handles herself and responds.

For example, I recently interviewed someone who told me that she lacked a specific skill I was seeking. However, her candor and explanation about how she'd overcome past shortcomings more than made up for the absence of this specific knowledge. So, develop a handful of questions that will provide a big-picture view—specific skills needed as well as critical insights about the candidate's attitude, resourcefulness, and integrity. I always like to ask, "If I were to speak with your last employer, what would she or he tell me was your greatest weakness? Strength?" Finally, pay attention to your intuition!

There's one additional alternative to hiring that's growing in popularity—outsourcing. By outsourcing, you can take advantage of an expert's skill set without directly employing them, and use them as much or as little as your business requires. This can be a great option for early-stage businesses that require certain expertise, such as marketing or accounting skills, but not on a full-time basis. It also eliminates the need for training, physical expansion, and management of day-to-day employee issues.

Tomima Edmark said that outsourcing employees was a key strategy as she grew her business. "You can get instant knowledge and be way ahead of the game rather than hiring and ramping up yourself," says Tomima. "I think outsourcing is always the way to go in the beginning, because you can get your capacity up immediately."

CREATING A COMPANY CULTURE

The great part about having your own business is that you are in charge of deciding whether to hire, whether to outsource, and how to establish standards of practice and quality that reflect your own beliefs. As an entrepreneur, your business is an outgrowth of you and your passion. Make it reflect your needs and personality.

"Even from my first little restaurant, I created systems and manuals and how-tos," says Madelyn Alfano. "The theory has always been if someone came from Mars and had to learn to wash dishes, I would hand them a manual and they would know exactly what to do."

She said she also takes the time to explain to employees the "whys" behind doing things, so they will understand and believe in what they're doing as much as she does.

Teri Gault created a tradition that brings fun into the workplace. When employees make a mistake, they are expected to write a limerick so that once the problem is solved, everyone can laugh it off. For example, when one employee failed to perform an important task— extracting key zip code data from an e-mail— here is the limerick he wrote to explain (and make light of) the situation:

> They said I had missed an extraction
> I replied with a surprised reaction
> "I'm sorry, Mrs. Gault
> But it was not my fault"
> Said I, "E-mail is a blasted contraption."

In running your own company, you also have the power to create an environment where employees can successfully combine family responsibilities with their career success. Being communicative and showing genuine concern for an employee's family or personal challenges is not antithetical to maintaining performance expectations and adherence to company policies.

However, you cannot let that genuine concern be detrimental to business success and growth. That's why it's so important to establish and communicate expectations from the beginning. In addition, you should give employees regular feedback on their performance. Further, if issues or conflicts with family responsibilities arise, there should be a formal process for discussing them. Or, if a company policy isn't working, discuss it to determine if it needs to change.

When considering employment policies, compensation programs, and other human resources decisions, there are a few basics to understand. From an article on Will Marre's Web site, www.american-dreamproject.org called, "The New Future: What's Driving An Invisible Movement That Will Change Everything," he points to a few key elements that affect employee satisfaction and productivity in today's world:

- Those surveyed value work that has meaning to them far above work that pays more.
- It takes about $50,000/year in family income for people to feel personally secure, meaning they can afford food, shelter, health care, and transportation.
- Commuting is the most stressful activity in most peoples' lives.

Think of what you can offer your employees to make their careers more meaningful, secure, and less stressful. Perhaps it's a decision-making voice or a small financial stake in the company, or the ability to use some aspect of their work time to help others. Or, structure their jobs to allow for flextime or telecommuting. Teri Gault, who still has virtually all her original employees, may hold the secret—every single one of them works from home. The Web-based nature of her business allows this, and she's found it works just fine.

MANAGE YOUR MANAGEMENT

All entrepreneurs can benefit from thoughtful management of two key areas—financials and personnel. A fundamental understanding of the important numbers, as well as a sharp awareness of how you'd like to choose and manage employees, can go a long way to helping you streamline your business and position it for stability and growth.

In the next chapter, we talk about overcoming adversity and finding personal inspiration. Most of the women I interviewed dealt with trying circumstances—both personally and professionally—and yet still managed to achieve business success. We will discover more about how they did it in Chapter 7 . . . and how they now feel compelled to give back.

Finding Strength:
Overcoming Adversity and
Giving Back

Media stories about entrepreneurs tend to focus on the people who have made it big. After all, have you ever seen a story about how hard it is for the entrepreneur slugging it out, day in and day out? When you see the spoils of success—a company that's already made it—you often don't hear about the tremendous hard work, challenging experiences, and exhaustion and fear that preceded success.

Like most entrepreneurs, almost all of the women in this book have encountered very serious business or personal obstacles that could have stopped them in their tracks . . . but didn't. Instead, they soldiered on. Some found inspiration in adversity, and some of them found solace from personal problems by redirecting pain or stress into a laser focus on their businesses. Others drew on their strength of entrepreneurship to get them through hard times. In addition, all of them, grateful for their success, have also been inspired to give back: to their communities, to their employees, and to their families.

THE DAILY GRIND

One of my roles during the last four years has been to encourage women to take chances and to find the courage to turn their ideas into tangible businesses. However, I would be remiss if I didn't share the fact that it involves hard work. And while I don't wish to discourage you, I think it's important that you understand from the outset the commitment it will take.

Some of these challenges include long hours, fatigue, stress, financial fear, and if you're a parent, the time it takes from your personal life—and the ongoing juggling act to ensure your children's needs are the priority. These have all been true for me in a big way. However, little has inspired me more than listening to the struggles and stories from the women featured in this book about how they dealt with hard work.

Maxine Clark, who worked her way up to the top of the corporate world before founding her own business, has never pretended success comes easily, especially if you plan to take your business to its farthest limits. When it comes to turning inspiration into action, Maxine believes the idea isn't the hard part. "There are a million ideas out there," she says. "The difference is in the implementation of those ideas . . . some of us have it and some of us don't. You need to know what your strengths are. I'm a great marketing person, a great implementer. I'm a great make-it-happen person, whatever it takes, 20 hours a day, 24 hours a day, nothing stops me. A lot of people are running their own business because they want to be independent, because they want to make their own hours—but they're not really looking to be a 200-store chain. And that's okay. But you have to decide whether you want to be a big fish in a small pond, or a small fish in a big pond."

Maxine says that running your own business is still a much bigger commitment than being a top executive in an established company. "You feel much more responsible," explains Maxine. "I have a lot less free time than I ever had working for somebody else. That's the myth—I think people think they're going to have a lot more flexibility [running their own business], but it depends on how serious you are. If you're going to build the business to its potential, then you're not going to have that luxury."

Although Karen Belasco has recently pared down her work hours to spend more time with her children, she still has a busy season that demands more of her time. "I do have more free time and flexibility . . . but I don't have ultimate freedom," she says. "There are demanding times during the year that I must be here more than my typical schedule. I have that responsibility, because it's my company and at the end of the day I am responsible for everything that goes on."

During the early stages of Airborne, Victoria Knight-McDowell's business, it was difficult to pinpoint where business stopped and her personal life began. She and her husband, Rider, often worked round-the-clock during crunch times to carry the business along. "The business was in the very small rental house we still lived in," she explains. "Accounting was in the back bedroom. Shipping and receiving was in the guest bedroom, until we had guests—then we'd get all the shippers off the bed. I also had 200 towers of shippers stacked in the hallway. We had a copy machine in the bathroom. Our bedroom and bathroom were the only rooms off-limits—actually, our bedroom was only off-limits after my eighth month of pregnancy. The dining room and living room were the main point of operations. When we would have a party, we'd just throw sheets over everything so you didn't see it and put up a card table with flowers and food."

When her baby was born, he had colic for the first three months, meaning Victoria was up most of the night. "When I nursed him and rocked him, he would sleep. As soon as I put him down, he'd wake up. So I would just take 1-800 calls all night. I was up anyway and holding him as he slept and I would just take the calls."

Teri Gault, too, said she vividly remembers the early stages of getting the business off the ground, when she and her husband were also having difficulties making ends meet. Her advice for others who want to take that first step? "Don't quit. Because that first year is tough. I really almost killed myself physically that first year. Thankfully I was desperate. Because if I hadn't been, with the three jobs and all the other stuff I was doing, I wouldn't have put the energy out like I did. I worked seven days a week, every day from morning until night—and into the night. I only slept a few hours a night. I figured out I made about 80 cents an hour that first year.

"But I would say right now as I sit here, I am so glad I didn't quit. And I probably would have, except the product was so good and the service was so good—people loved it so much, so that's what kept me going."

Unfortunately, the grueling pace doesn't end after the first year. In fact, things became even more challenging for Victoria Knight-McDowell as Airborne grew. That was the primary reason why she and her husband decided to pursue venture capitalists to invest in the company and take over the day-to-day affairs of the business.

As she explains, "It got too big. That last year was so intense—it was so incredibly intense—we were getting sick. It was so worrisome. My husband did not sleep for a year. And even afterward, he was so wound up it was almost like posttraumatic stress syndrome. We were just so wired our adrenaline was going, going, going."

BUSINESS CURVE BALLS

In addition to the daily grind and the grueling schedules that just about every entrepreneur experiences, many have also contended with seemingly insurmountable business hurdles—challenges that would have caused the faint of heart simply to close up shop. Yet our business-moms showed the power of perseverance, creativity, and overcoming adversity.

Victoria Knight-McDowell faced a major unexpected hurdle early in the business. She had just landed her first big drugstore account. To promote the product in-store and get the word out about the Airborne product, the chain agreed to give out special promotional postcards with samples attached to it—a great opportunity. But there was an error in the postcard printing. And by the time it was fixed and new postcards were shipped to them, Victoria had less than a week to attach 44,000 samples, by hand, to the preprinted postcard . . . and she was still working full time as a teacher!

To start this monumental task, "Rider and I timed ourselves to see how long it would take to do one crate," she explains. "It took us three hours, the two of us, to do 1,700 of them. I was in such a panic. I got to school first thing in the morning and I put a big note on the bulletin board to ask for help. I had boxes of them in the back of my Blazer—it was like dealing in the parking lot! The librarian took some home for her kids to do. The woman who ran the computer lab had her teenage kids do some. The gal who ran the cheerleading program had all the girls do it to earn money.

"So we got it done. We're meeting people in parking lots and transporting all this stuff from one car to another—it was mind-boggling. And Rider and I were up until two in the morning counting, sticking loose samples back on, and stacking them a certain way. We learned all about how to stack and ship and do pallets and that sort of thing!"

Victoria also experienced financial strains as well. When a national retail drugstore chain ordered $750,000 in product—bigger than any order she'd ever received—it seemed like a great opportunity. The downside was that they would only pay for what was sold, when it sold, and that it drained her inventory almost entirely.

"We had to beg, borrow, and steal to fill our other orders, and then this money would just dribble in," explains Victoria. We had also committed to doing $25,000 or $50,000 in advertising—our first national campaign, we had to do it. That was a very, very hard year— I had to work with our vendors, paying them off a little at a time. And they weren't happy about it. In the beginning they were flexible, and then as it went on and on they got testier. That was our biggest lesson. After that, we learned to say no. A buy is a buy. We were naïve."

When someone like Victoria speaks of long hours and financial stress, I really understand. For me, as rewarding as my own business has been, collectively there have been months of sleepless nights. The reality of having two babies when launching the company certainly increased my challenge. Our challenges have also included the countless times we have ended the week with our energy reserve on empty, combined with the stress of not knowing how we would finance the next week's business requirements or pay our personal mortgages and the girls' preschool fees.

Even when an entrepreneur has a supportive spouse or partner, it can be a lonely experience. It's like playing dodge ball in elementary school—the minute you've avoided one problem thrown at you, the next one is being hurled your way. And, it's not just problems—it's the number of unexpected things that come each day (by phone, e-mail, and fax) that can be both positive and negative but that require thought and time. Sometimes, I feel like shouting, "Incoming!"

For example, one Sunday night we learned by e-mail that our entire inventory in a Los Angeles warehouse was padlocked by the police. This inventory included an enormous new shipment that had arrived from China two days earlier, as well as three of our largest customers' orders that were packed and waiting for UPS to pick up and deliver. We later learned that the owner of our third-party warehouse had not paid his rent for months! Our biggest customer was awaiting a shipment and we had no access to our inventory. It took over a week to uncover who even owned the building and another three weeks, two flights made by my husband to Los Angeles, hiring a lawyer, serious diplomacy, and thousands of dollars (a scarcity at the time) to ameliorate the situation and gain access to our entire inventory—not to mention a search for a new warehouse.

The Sunday night e-mail came in to our office while I was on a flight to Dallas, Texas, for an early Monday morning television appearance, which was part of the tour for my first published book. I learned of the situation minutes before I had to go on the air live, knowing that we could be out of business if we couldn't get our hands on our inventory. In fact, before things were negotiated, we were told that the owner of the building now technically owned our inventory since his tenant (our warehouse vendor) hadn't paid his rent even though we had paid him on time each month. You can imagine how I was *really* feeling when I had to go on air, smiling, as if nothing was wrong—providing viewers tips about how they, too, could become an entrepreneur. I felt that I had earned an Academy Award!

Mary Micucci of Along Came Mary Productions is no stranger to pressure, either. For her, it's pretty much a daily fact of life—or at least of doing business—when dealing with celebrities and other Hollywood power brokers who make up her primary clientele.

"Stress can be the downside of success for any business owner. When you work at a high level," Mary says, "and you are a perfectionist, and you know things have to be the best for your clients, it can become overwhelming. We all know that any successful person needs to manage stress. I've learned to do this with a good diet, exercise, a sound vitamin regimen, and most importantly by creating quality down time."

Madelyn Alfano also experienced extreme challenges. "In 1994 we had the earthquake" she remembers. "I lost my biggest (in sales) restaurant—Woodland Hills—and my Sherman Oaks restaurant was also destroyed. And we were just opening in Northridge, the heart of the earthquake, a block away from where an apartment building collapsed."

In addition, Madelyn experienced several difficulties in her personal life. As she explains, "It was one of my toughest years, actually. My uncle had had a stroke and was in a coma, and I was the fiduciary responsible for his day-to-day care. So for seven months I was trying to rebuild Woodland Hills and Sherman Oaks. I was building the new business in Northridge, and most of the area was devastated. Every day I'd pick up my mom, take her to the hospital, run to the restaurant, then go back to the hospital at night to take her home. Meanwhile I was rebuilding the other two restaurants. It was a very intense year."

Lane Nemeth also had "one of those years" that could have stopped her in her tracks and put her out of business. "The toughest time I ever had in my life was in 1983, when the business had reached the ten million dollar mark," Lane says. "My venture capitalist informed me that this was the time when most entrepreneurs lost their businesses, and advised me to make massive changes to management. So I hired a CEO and I spent the next year pretty much letting him run the business, which, frankly, I was happy to do because I was so tired, just exhausted. So I spent a great deal of time in the field, motivating and listening and inspiring, and it was wonderful. But when I looked at my September financial statements, we had lost a significant amount of money, which had never happened before.

"I asked my CEO what happened and he gave me all these reasons why we really weren't in trouble—he said everything had a very legitimate reason. And I bought it. And the next month, October, I discovered we were in an even bigger loss position. And the bank called me that same day and said they were pulling out our loan. So now I have an $800,000 loss, no capital, and no bank. And I thought that meant I was out of business. I felt like a Mack truck had hit me, that we're out of business and that we're going to lose our house. I just wanted to sleep.

"The next day, though, something came to me. I can only call it divine inspiration. I had this image of my daughter in an intensive care ward. And I wondered if I'd be lying there in bed, doing nothing about it. No! I'd be yelling and screaming at every doctor trying to find where I could get her fixed! If I had any control helping her get better, I'd do it. Then I had another vision—I was on stage, telling the 5,000 women who worked for Discovery Toys that I was tired, I didn't feel like doing this any more, that I wasn't adequate for the job. I knew I couldn't do that, either. So I put on a business suit and I walked into the office and I fired that CEO—I just said, 'Get out of my building, get out of my life!'—and I pulled together the team and I laid out the financials. And I called my accounting firm and asked them to send me the biggest, fanciest, most wonderful CFO that they've ever heard of."

Lane said that the new CFO was the company's saving grace. He helped arrange for a loan with a new bank, and also helped solve another potentially business-busting obstacle when Lane's computer system failed, by talking a friend into loaning the company $1 million for the massive systems upgrade it needed. Once the CFO had all systems back on track in about one year's time he died suddenly, leaving Lane stunned and grief stricken. She remembers him as being one of the most incredible human beings in her life.

Karen Belasco shared an experience that affected both her business and personal life, when someone she trusted completely betrayed her. "I hired a caretaker/nanny for my children who stayed with me at the factory during the day," she explains. "When they reached preschool age, off they went. The nanny had recently graduated college and asked if she could help out. I told her I needed an extra Cookie Counselor on the phones and someone to reach out to the media. She was smart and caught on quickly.

"One day, a couple years later, she announced she was leaving to pursue other endeavors. She did, in fact, leave—to pursue the same exact business it had taken me years to build. There was absolutely nothing I could do. I could have gone to court, but at a minimum I was looking at facing a quarter of a million dollars and the next four years of my life. Not really an option.

"I was mad, outraged, pissed, upset, but as the old saying goes . . . what doesn't kill you, makes you stronger. And it has made me stronger. Since her departure, there's been a real fire in my belly. I had to differentiate myself from her and everyone else, re-creating Good Fortunes so that we'd continue to be number one in our market. We created new product lines, some successful and some not. But there isn't a day that goes by that I'm not thinking of something new and different—and now, with perspective, I have her to thank!"

REAL LIFE DOESN'T STOP

Of course, solving problems is part of business—even when the unexpected occurs. When personal problems occur at the same time, though, it can weigh heavily on an entrepreneur who's already overburdened by the demands of her business. Unfortunately, few are immune from life's personal hurdles, and our Millionaire Moms are no exception. Collectively, they've come through some of life's most difficult personal issues—illnesses, divorce, and the deaths of loved ones. Along with facing ongoing business challenges and endless work hours, they also managed personal crises.

Maria Sobrino recalls two events that changed the direction of her life significantly—expanding her travel company from Mexico to California, and her divorce. She says, "I had always been curious about the United States and I saw an opportunity to expand to the Los Angeles area. Unfortunately, at the same time, I was not happy in my marriage. I tried to find happiness there for several years until I understood it was holding up my life. So I had to have the courage to ask for a divorce—no matter what the consequences. I dedicated myself to starting Lulu's Dessert Corporation—and put all my energy and the best I had to give to learn more, every day." Her business became a diversion from the difficulties in her personal life.

THE INSIDE STORY

Victoria Knight-McDowell

Victoria Knight-McDowell was a second-grade teacher in Carmel, California, who often brought home more than papers to grade—she also brought back germs and illnesses that she caught from her students.

So she set out to create a natural formula that would give her body a fighting chance against germs. She started by researching Chinese and holistic medicine and the use of herbs and vitamins to boost the immune system. She was also inspired by the homemade herbal remedies her mother brewed to maintain her family's health.

She continued working with nutrition experts and herbalists until she found the right blend of 17 ingredients, including herbal extracts, vitamins, electrolytes, amino acids, and antioxidants. This formula became Airborne (www.airbornehealth.com).

She launched Airborne in 1997 with her husband, Rider. Through a homespun marketing campaign and ample word of mouth, it soon became an American phenomenon. Drug stores around the country began selling it, celebrities began endorsing it of their own volition, and sales grew from $25,000 in 1997 to $145 million in 2005, after less than 10 years in business.

She and her husband worked day and night during this period to keep up with the demand. At the same time, Victoria had a baby boy. She always encouraged and maintained a family-friendly atmosphere as her company grew from its first location in their small home to its current space.

Today, Airborne continues to grow in popularity and the product line consists of seven varieties for adults and children.

© Photo credit: John Todd

Other epiphanies also influenced her as she started her business. "My mom and dad in Mexico didn't believe I was going to make it in a new country," she explains. "That gave me the courage that my decision to go into business would be successful, despite all the events I was going through. I just couldn't give up, and I do not know the word 'failure.' It took 11 years for my dad to recognize that I was seriously in business . . . and I won the battle. It was a blessing for me."

Debi Davis, too, kept the company going while managing her family as a single mom although it wasn't always easy. She ended up learning lessons along the way—lessons she now passes on, through example, to her children. "I think that there was a benefit in that both of my kids are very conscientious and quite entrepreneurial," says Debi. "But there was a point when my business took a huge amount of time, especially since I didn't have a life partner. Being a single mom and running a $45 million company was really tough. Even though my ex-husband was still very active with my family, you're still the mom. And watching mom's life wasn't very fun in relation to watching dad's life, who had lots of dates and girlfriends. But in the last five years my day pretty much ends at five and my weekends are for my kids, and I think it's really paid off. They recognize that there are times when an eight-hour day isn't enough, but they also understand there are other obligations and you have to balance them out."

For Rachel Ashwell, starting and running Shabby Chic was a way to manage her personal responsibilities and the demands of motherhood. "My babies were tiny," remembers Rachel. "I had a newborn—two-weeks-old—and a two-year-old baby. I felt I needed to have a business that would allow me to control my hours. If I had had some big thought that I'm going to start this furniture store and it's going to grow so much, I probably wouldn't have done it. I took on mismatched partners and lost tons of money and wondered how I got there. But the good news is that I also said yes to a lot of things. So you jump on opportunities . . . but you also make some wrong decisions.

"What's kept me going is that I've had a really good life," Rachel continues. "I'm healthy, my kids are great. But I definitely feel like business is where I've placed my passions in life . . . other dreams, personal dreams, haven't necessarily gone sometimes as I thought they would. But rather than mope around, I've just thrown my creativity into my business. I think some of my best works have been during the sadder times in my life, which is kind of interesting."

Perhaps Madelyn Alfano had the greatest difficulties when she faced the unthinkable—her son's genetic disability and fight for achieving a "normal" life, which ended in 2000. Max had been born in 1988, the same year that she opened her second restaurant. Remembering this difficult time, Madelyn explains, "When my first son Max was born, I was told he was perfect. Then at three months I noticed that his eyes were moving back and forth like a cuckoo clock. The doctor told me after a half-hour exam that Max was blind and had a genetic birth defect. He said we needed specialized tests to be sure. The drive home from this appointment seemed very long. I was alone in my car, wondering how I could break this news to my parents, who were waiting at my house to hang out with Max. That night my entire family was at my house as if someone had died. I realized then that I needed to get up the next day and make things happen for Max.

"After several tests and referrals, a doctor of genetics diagnosed Max as being severely mentally retarded, and told us we should consider putting him in a home. I could not believe what I was hearing. How could this beautiful boy with curly blond hair and blue eyes and an infectious laugh be put away? I got up, walked outside and sat on the curb. Max's dad came out and said to me, 'You better sell your restaurants because you are going to need all your time to take care of Max.'

"Ten restaurants later, I can tell you that I did not take the doctor's, or Max's father's, advice," she continues. "I spent years devoted to giving Max unconditional love and finding the best specialists available to help him develop to the best of his ability. The experts at UCLA were astonished with his progress. Everyone doesn't operate at the same level. Max struggled so hard to learn simple tasks, like picking up his head and closing his mouth to chew.

"Any business problem I'd come up against would be laughable by comparison. I realized that there are no serious business problems that could not be solved. I also became an extremely patient person. Before Max, I expected everyone to learn as fast as I did, and when someone didn't get it I was frustrated. Helping Max in his development meant breaking down every task into many steps. Jobs offered in the restaurant industry are first-time opportunities for many entering the workforce. I want everyone who works at Maria's to be successful, which means it's important for me to provide the proper tools and education that allows them to achieve that goal. I treat everyone as if they are family."

For Jeanne Bice, her husband's death changed everything, giving her the impetus—and inspiration—to launch The Quacker Factory. "Suddenly, I had to make a living," Jeanne remembers. "I hit rock bottom, I was either going to die or get better. I was just this pampered little housewife, and all of a sudden I didn't have a pot to piss in. I had nothing. I had to figure out how to earn a living. And that motivates you to take your business to greatness."

MILLION-DOLLAR SECRET

"You can have a business and you can make just enough money to hang on," says Jeanne Bice, "but one day you become very tired when you realize you're killing yourself just to hang on. That's not the purpose of life or the purpose of business. If you're going to be in business, it should take you to glory."

For Deann Murphy, too, life's difficulties prompted her to start her business. She is a true example of the saying, "when one door closes, another opens." As she tells the story, "A girlfriend and I were quilt makers by hobby. And a friend of ours was having a baby, so we wanted to make a quilt for her. It was 1972. I had just lost my job at Columbia University. They had closed down the research center I was working in. I was also going through a difficult personal loss at the time. So I was able to be home with my friend, doing this quilt, when I wouldn't normally have been able to do that. And we said, gee, you know, I bet that other people would like to be able to make these quilts, but they're really hard to do. But they had so much value— they were art pieces, they were heirlooms, they were pieces of

American history. All of this came together when we were talking about making a quilt for our friend. And we said, 'Hey, what about making quilt kits? Wouldn't that be a cool product?' My girlfriend was willing to try this adventure with me and it all happened at a moment in time."

Terrie Williams experienced a "crippling episode of depression." As she tells it publicly, " . . . you know I represented Puffy and Janet Jackson, Eddie Murphy, and all these different people, yes, that's true, but let me tell you about the nine months when I could barely get out of bed." As Terrie explains, "I did what I had to do. What I could summon up the strength and the energy to do. It wasn't just what I was going through, waking up with that crippling anxiety and all the other things. It was having to walk out the door with *the* face, dying inside! There were some days, it was like, 'Oh my God, I can't do this.' But I had a business to run. I had a speaking engagement. And, sometimes the tears would flow just before getting ready to go. But I would walk out that door, walk into that thing with the game face on, and I would literally have a moment and say, 'is this the person that was just at the house?' Crumpled on the floor, yeah, that was me."

Terrie's new book, *Black Pain*, is scheduled to be released at the end of 2007 and is being considered a landmark book on the subject matter of black people and mental health.

As children, both Teri Gault and Kathy Gendel experienced life-changing events that they credit with motivating and strengthening them, even today. For Teri, the single event that changed the direction of her life happened when she was 13 years old. "Our house burned to the ground while we were in it, at 2 a.m.," she says. "We barely got out alive. I ran through flames and my hair was singed. I had to have it cut short because of it. I was in junior high and had always worried about how I looked and what people thought. But this experience stripped me of everything on the exterior, and it also stripped me of possessions. My worldview shifted dramatically, as I found value in people and life rather than things.

"I felt I had experienced something that changed my life for the better. And that I could survive anything. When going through terrible financial times as an adult, my dad used to say, 'The last chapter hasn't been written.' I pondered that a lot. And now that I am through some of those other times, I am more aware than ever that what we have now can change . . . even overnight. When things are bad, I believe 100 percent that they can change for the better."

As a girl, Kathy Gendel of Breezies Intimates was extremely close to her grandmother. Today, her life's work allows her to honor her memory . . . and her grandmother's battle with breast cancer. "My true inspiration for everything I do today is my dear grandmother," says Kathy. "Everything was grand about her. She was a milliner and an excellent seamstress, so she was always flamboyantly dressed from head to toe. She developed breast cancer 40 years ago when chemotherapy was not an option. The doctor gave her six months to live, and she lived 11 years. Every day I'd watch her maneuver this rather large, obtrusive bra to make her prosthetic enhancer fit just right. She was always in a great deal of pain, but nothing slowed her down. This made such an impression on me at age 10 that I knew then I'd become involved in finding a cure for this cruel, ravaging disease."

Watching her grandmother go through this experience influenced Kathy's business tremendously. "I hold a patent for two different types of pockets in a mastectomy bra," she explains. "The Gendel family is also very involved in finding a cure for breast cancer through large donations to various cancer research foundations and Race for the Cure. I think when you are a family of girls, the heightened awareness is tenfold."

FINDING INSPIRATION

Sharing stories of the personal adversity of highly effective women can be a valuable learning tool for all of us. It demands that one give up the illusions and judgments about others based on their financial wealth. Although they run successful businesses, the moms in this book deal with business and personal problems like anyone else, and yet have come through to the other side—stronger and more successful for it.

I asked each of them if there was a quote, story, song, or prayer—or another source of inspiration—that helped them persevere through the toughest times. This is what they shared with me:

Victoria Knight-McDowell of Airborne goes back, again and again, to this Goethe quote when things get rocky:

"Be bold and mighty forces will come to your aid."

She says that often in her business, when a problem or setback seemed insurmountable, an even better solution would present itself, and that this quote epitomizes her experience.

Terrie Williams, who speaks to audiences about her experiences, says, "I have to remind myself to push through the fear 10 times a day. It is as Eleanor Roosevelt said, 'You must do the very thing you are afraid to do.'"

Her relationship with God has been her primary source of guidance. "I think many people are not still enough to listen to the inner voice that always tells you what to do, where to go, and how to do it."

Among the quotes she uses for inspiration comes this one from the *Daily Prayer & Promises Devotional Journal for Every Day*, Barbour Publishing:

"My child, whenever you encounter an obstacle, remember, I have already provided a way around it or through it. The next time you see a cloud on the horizon, don't fear the storm. Look closely, and you will see and feel My presence."

Kathy Gendel finds herself quoting her grandmother on a regular basis. "My grandmother talked in clichés and metaphors. I think it was just that era," Kathy explains. "'Four eyes are better than two,'

'When God gives a lot, he expects a lot,' and her favorite was 'them who has, gets.' I live my life paraphrasing all her little sayings every day, and my girls do exactly the same."

Deann Murphy says that the Serenity Prayer, in particular, helps her be calm and focused at the same time. She finds herself reciting it in her mind at least 10 times a day. It helped her handle business challenges ranging from hiring, firing, and discerning what, in life, is worthwhile, and what things are a waste of time.

SERENITY PRAYER

God grant me the serenity to accept the things I cannot change,
the courage to change the things I can,
and the wisdom to know the difference.

Maria Sobrino finds herself praying to the Virgin Mary for help and inspiration. "I pray for my daughters and my mother's love and support from Mexico to keep me going. My faith and hope have been strong all my life."

Maria also shared two additional quotes that she frequently goes back to:

"Life isn't about finding yourself. Life is about creating yourself."

and

"Happiness is a journey, not a destination."

Karen Belasco finds ongoing inspiration in a quote by Herman Cain:

"Success is not the key to happiness. Happiness is the key to success. If you love what you are doing, you will be successful."

Maxine Clark says that "The Golden Rule" has always served her well. Her mother shared it with her early in life.

"Treat others as you would like to be treated." (The Golden Rule is a fundamental moral principle found in virtually all major religions and cultures—source: Wikipedia)

"My mother used to remind me of it and it is always there for me to lean on—it is always the right thing to do!"

Teri Gault says that the Psalms in the Bible never fail to put things in perspective for her, especially Psalm 121, A Song of Ascents. During her toughest financial times and when she underwent the exhausting hours of getting The Grocery Game off the ground, she would sometimes go outside, look at the mountains near her home, and recite it to find strength:

I will lift up my eyes to the hills—
From whence comes my help?
My help comes from the Lord,
Who made heaven and earth.

He will not allow your foot to be moved;
He who keeps you will not slumber.
Behold, he who keeps Israel
Shall neither slumber nor sleep.

The Lord is your keeper
The Lord is your shade at your right hand.
The sun shall not strike you by day,
Nor the moon by night.

The Lord shall preserve you from all evil;
He shall preserve your soul.
The Lord shall preserve your going out and your coming in
From this time forth, and even forevermore.

Madelyn Alfano shared two sources of strength and inspiration. The first, simply called "Smile," she found framed and hanging on the wall of her grandmother's apartment in Hoboken, New Jersey, during a 1985 visit. While the author is unknown, it is believed to be based on the writings of Rabbi Samson Rafael Hirsch (1808–1888). The minute she saw it, she knew she had to add it to her employee handbook. Madelyn says she tries to model this behavior every day. It starts like this:

SMILE

"A smile costs nothing, but gives much. It enriches those who receive it, without making poorer those who give. It takes but a moment, but the memory of it sometimes lasts forever."

The full poem can be found at www.mominventors.com/millionairemoms.

Madelyn also shares another source of strength. An excerpt from a poem called "Today I Will Make a Difference" by Max Lucado, an award-winning Christian writer and pastor.

TODAY I WILL MAKE
A DIFFERENCE

" . . . Today I will make a difference.

I will be grateful for the twenty-four hours that are before me. Time is a precious commodity. I refuse to allow what little time I have to be contaminated by self-pity, anxiety or boredom.

I will face this day with the joy of a child and the courage of a giant. I will drink each minute as though it is my last. When tomorrow comes, today will be gone forever. While it is here, I will use it for loving and giving . . . "

To learn more about Max Lucado's work please visit: www.maxlucado.com.

THE INSIDE STORY

Mary Micucci

In the mid-1970s, Mary Micucci started a small catering company from the back of her Volkswagen Bug. After a small but high-profile dinner party she catered, word of mouth spread immediately. Her head for business and people-oriented personality helped her grow the business, Along Came Mary Productions, into what it is today—the number-one event coordinating and gourmet catering company in southern California.

Her groundbreaking style of producing events has revolutionized her industry. She's been dubbed "the Epicurean Steven Spielberg" for creating ultra-creative and glamorous events that aren't soon forgotten, including countless movie premiere galas and creative corporate events for Fortune 500 clientele.

In the meantime, she raised her daughter, now 20-years-old.

"It's a juggling act when you're growing a business," said Mary. "But as a family we were very committed to be there for her because she was a blessing. I was an older parent, and to me she was a miracle."

In fact it is Mary's own family—her brother and sister—who inspired her to start the business and create her success. Her older sister, who helped raise Mary after her mother died, taught her the importance of holidays and traditions and food. Her brother, a trained French chef and majordomo to New York City's wealthiest households, mentored and watched over her growing business.

Today she's hosting spectacular premiere parties for major Hollywood movies like *Harry Potter*, *Batman*, and *Charlie's*

Angels, celebrity-filled Emmy and Grammy Award show parties, and major corporate events for clients like Coca-Cola, ABC, and Universal Studios.

Her secret?

"Just go for it. You really don't have anything to lose," said Mary. "And if you decide it's not what you want, don't beat yourself up, because there are other opportunities in life."

© Photo credit: Mark Elkins

GIVING BACK MAKES THEM STRONGER

While inspiration came from various individuals and spiritual sources, like those shared in the previous section, for most of these women, inspiration also comes through action: specifically, through giving. In addition to overcoming their own personal hardships and finding outside guidance for inspiration, most of the women I interviewed reported finding their greatest strength and reward in giving back. For some, that means giving people a good working environment and opportunities they might otherwise not have had. For others, it means contributing money and time to causes close to their hearts. And for most of them, it's both.

Lane Nemeth explains that being a successful entrepreneur is an incredibly powerful vehicle for giving. A profitable, successful business empowers entrepreneurs to give more than they may have ever thought possible. She puts it this way, "Some people say to me, 'I want to rescue dogs.' I say great. You can only own two, three, four dogs safely. But if you have money, you can maybe own a farm in Montana and rescue a thousand dogs. But you can't do it if you can't afford to feed them." Lane's own desire to offer products to animal owners that pets would love led her to start Petlane.

"I think it's a question of finding something you're passionate about. I am so passionate about animals, I just love them. But I'm even more passionate about helping people achieve their dreams. The most incredible thing in the whole world is to watch somebody become successful and know that you had a hand in it."

Lane touches upon a common thread among women business owners. In particular, this group seems more invested in their employees' success and well-being. Maxine Clark is driven similarly. "What motivates me today," she explains, "is mostly the success of other people—seeing other people be able to realize their dreams and their aspirations through this company and seeing kids feel important when they come to the store. At this point in my life, it's about giving back to the community and making a difference that lasts way beyond my time on this earth."

Making money has allowed her to give back and change the lives of others. Maxine says, "I have been able to be a much more charitable person because of the wealth created from Build-A-Bear Workshop. I am asked to speak at universities and high schools, and many budding entrepreneurs contact me on a daily basis for advice. I wrote my book in order to spread the ability to dream."

For Karen Belasco, creating a positive work environment is a key goal of her business. According to her, "We've created a family and not just a place to work. Not that we're all friends and know everyone else's business, but we're all concerned coworkers. We've had at least 20 children born while I've been in business, and most of the women and men still work here today. Together we've been through births, birthdays, starting school and graduations, weddings, divorces, and deaths. Even the ones who've chosen different career paths still come to visit or call."

In addition to having more resources now to support various charitable organizations, Teri Gault also finds satisfaction in the very nature of her business, which helps others "pay it forward." She loves getting e-mail from people who explain how The Grocery Game has benefited them. "I have helped them to feed their families, and now they are able to donate to food pantries. This thrills me more than anything. I know what I do is good for my own family, but when I realize I am affecting other lives in a positive way it has eternal meaning for me."

These amazing businesswomen also provide financial support to charities ranging from breast cancer to children's organizations to culture and the arts. It brings joy to them to be able to use their creativity to help others. Jeanne Bice has one unique tradition she's carried on that has really allowed her to do neat things. It grew out of what she went through during her own difficult times.

As she explains, "I've never been a go-to-church and volunteer for Sunday School kind of person—because I'm not good at that. But when I was in a bad position and I just didn't know what I was going to do, people helped me. One day a friend just handed me a check for $5,000 and told me, 'I don't want it back. Use it.'

"And I did. Now I call it my 'Leg Up' fund. And when I see that somebody just needs a leg up, they're still at that rock-and-a-hard-place time, I write them a check and say, 'I don't want you to ever talk about it, I don't want it back—but when you're back on your feet, pass it on to somebody else who needs a leg up.' I did pay my initial money back for my own pride. But I've also passed it on. I believe you need to spread your wealth."

Because she is one of the country's most successful Latina woman business owners, Maria Sobrino finds herself in a different position to give—as a role model. Maria believes, "Giving back to the community is very, very important. Because as Latinas, we don't share. This is something I want to change—we are a very jealous culture, everything is 'my, my, my' and 'I'm not going to tell you how I did it.' But it doesn't take us anywhere. We need to teach the next generation to work as a team and share information. And because I know where I come from and I know how difficult it is, I want to fight to have more women involved in business."

Terrie Williams gives back in nearly everything she does including a cautionary note about giving to ourselves. "Giving away too much of yourself, not putting the oxygen mask over your own mouth first is the biggest casualty. If there's a need for oxygen, when the mask comes down, put it over your own mouth first."

MILLION-DOLLAR SECRET

"As I learned to do business in the United States," shares Maria, "all my experiences have made me learn how important it is to share and give back. Being a mentor and sharing experiences is the best gift a leader can give."

Madelyn Alfano is extremely well known in her community as a giver. She is involved in numerous children's charities, including a major project started in her late son Max's honor to build handicapped dorms at a large California science camp—www.bluesky meadow.org. She donates over 60 restaurant gift certificates each week to various charities. She also gives her time to fundraisers and to friends and family who are in need. She explains, candidly, that there is also an unfortunate downside to giving.

"I get to spend a lot of time on philanthropy," says Madelyn. "I get to make a difference in our community because I've built a big enough infrastructure where I don't have to be in the restaurants every day. I feel very blessed that I can do this through being a successful businesswoman." But, she continues, "I get hundreds of invitations to very expensive events. My CFO put me on a philanthropy budget because I give too much."

Perhaps the most valuable aspect of being an entrepreneur—especially once the business is off the ground—is the ability to control your time, your schedule, and your life. Madelyn Alfano speaks for many of the women I interviewed when she explains the value this freedom allows—whether it's giving to charitable organizations, or to one's own family and friends.

"Entrepreneurship has afforded me the time to be present wherever I am needed," says Madelyn. "It is definitely a vehicle for finding a higher meaning in life. After all, where else can you earn a great living, have time to spend with your family and friends, and also be an active part of the community? Owning my own business gives me the opportunity to control my own schedule. The freedom of time is a most precious commodity and should not be abused or wasted."

Perhaps, in the end, this is what we are all after—more time. Although it takes a great deal of time and hard work in the beginning, as many of the women explained earlier in this chapter, entrepreneurship can eventually give us more of our most limited commodity. Former teacher Victoria Knight-McDowell, who no longer runs the day-to-day affairs for Airborne, now has the time to make an impact in other ways—by volunteering her time at her son's school, by helping oversee an Airborne company trust that awards grants to teachers, and by having time to spend with her extended family across the country.

Terrie Williams started the Stay Strong Foundation for youth offering workshops and mentoring opportunities for at-risk kids and ex-offenders across the country. In addition, by leveraging her background as a social worker, as a sufferer of depression, and as a public relations person, she has made it her personal mission to raise awareness about mental health issues, particularly among the black community.

Julie Clark, who sold Baby Einstein, now has the freedom to spend more time with her family. She also used proceeds from her first company to found The Safe Side, which helps keep children safe from predators, a cause very close to her heart. Opening this new business has allowed her not only to have a great impact on the safety of children but it's allowed her to achieve her own dream of helping others.

"My dream now," says Julie, "is to get an e-mail from a mom who says her kid didn't get in a car [with a stranger] because he watched my video. To change somebody's life is a way bigger dream than to make more money. The money [from Baby Einstein] is fantastic, and it's helped me have dreams that aren't money-related. If you have no money, you're always dreaming of having more money and that's the reality of everybody's life. You always want to be able to provide for your family. I guess now that I've achieved it, I think my dreams can be broader and more philanthropic than they would have been if I was just struggling to make ends meet for my own family."

MILLION-DOLLAR SECRET

"I think it's wonderful to dream of success," says Julie Clark, "because if you have good, positive dreams, then you're in the right place. If you can do it in a way that's healthy, and that doesn't take away from the things that are most precious—your children and your family—it's fantastic."

After selling her company, which she had run for 25 years, Deann Murphy had the time to turn to philanthropic ventures, as well. She now spends at least half her time volunteering for not-for-profit organizations. She serves as chair for the Women's Business Development Center in Stamford, Connecticut, where she lends her experience to help other women entrepreneurs, is on the board of the Center for Women's Business Research, and is also vice-chair of a local hospital.

"It makes it all worthwhile," Deann explains. "It's just highly satisfying. I love working to help entrepreneurs find their own success. You're giving people a way to support themselves and unleash their creativity. You're creating jobs for people. That's what it means to me."

The reality is that success increases one's ability to create more life choices. And for many women, that means the ability to give. Nell Merlino, who runs the "Make Mine a Million Business™" program that provides micro-loans, mentoring, and marketing to female entrepreneurs, says that when they apply for loans, none of the women ever say that making money is their primary goal. Rather, money is more of a means to an end.

"I wish more young women appreciated that if they all ran hedge funds, they could probably do more to save the world," Nell explains. "They could spend six months working, and six months helping in Darfur or wherever they wanted to help. It's so interesting."

In other words, the opportunities of successful entrepreneurship are basically endless. Will Marre, who created the American Dream Project (www.americandreamproject.org)—a national educational initiative and a community of change leaders designed to reignite the real American Dream—talks of the importance of a dream and of giving.

American Dream Project

"The world will change when your world changes. The world needs your dream. Thomas Jefferson declared the American Dream when he called for life, liberty, and the pursuit of happiness. The American Dream is more than the opportunity to shop at the mall and pursue whatever pleasure is in fashion," explains Marre on his Web site.

He continues by saying that you can find happiness by creating personal meaning in your life—and that giving is an excellent way to achieve it. "The quality of our future depends on you," Marre says. "It depends on each one of us. When we make higher choices, we are giving a gift to all who are affected. When we stand for ideals, or contribute new ideas, we give our unique gift. Something no one else can duplicate. The future is changed when enough of us exercise the courage to give. Now is the time."

In the next and final chapter we'll talk more about just what achieving that dream takes—and what traits many of our Millionaire Moms share.

Achieving Success:
What Does It Take?

Through talking with aspiring entrepreneurs on an almost daily basis, and going through the entrepreneurial process myself, I have discovered something interesting—there is a mystique associated with launching one's own business. Simply said, many people believe that successful entrepreneurs are born with specific personality traits that others don't have. This mystique leads to certain myths that can dampen a prospective entrepreneur's enthusiasm, so in this chapter I'd like to explain and debunk some of the more common misperceptions.

At the same time, I've also discovered that there are, indeed, certain behaviors and traits that *can* aid an entrepreneur's success. Many of our Millionaire Moms share common attitudes, work ethics, or ways of thinking about things, and credit these factors to helping them find success. I will share these with you, too—to help you tap into your own strengths and beliefs in order to find your way.

First, let's explore some common myths about what breeds success.

DEBUNKING THE MYTHS

Many people believe they don't have the innate qualities necessary to find success as an entrepreneur, and that self-made millionaires are somehow "different" from them. I think that many of the most commonly held beliefs, however, are simply myths, and our Millionaire Moms' experiences support my position. In this section, I discredit five common myths about successful entrepreneurs.

MYTH NO. 1: YOU HAVE TO BE "MS. PERSONALITY"

Reality: People with many different personality types have become successful. For as many outgoing Martha Stewarts and Richard Bransons, there are countless successful entrepreneurs with very low profiles who wish to stay that way. It's more important to be smart in business and to build a strong team than it is to be charismatic.

It's also helpful to learn from others' examples.

"I study successful people. Because one day it occurred to me, they started out just like me," explained Jeanne Bice. "I've heard that Martha Stewart started out selling pies in front of a Ralph Lauren store in a strip mall. From humble beginnings she became a great success. To this day I read about people who have become successful, and I use people as role models. And I look at success, I don't look at failures. Because I'm not headed for a failure."

MYTH NO. 2: THE IDEA IS THE MOST IMPORTANT THING

Reality: Yes, it's important to have a good idea. But that's not even half the battle. More important is how you position your product or service, and how it meets your target market's needs. You don't need to invent something completely novel, like the iPod or microwave oven, to be successful—you can also take an idea that already exists and simply make it better.

Case in point: Maxine Clark didn't invent teddy bears—and she's the first person who'll tell you that. She did, however, invent something special—an emotional experience and connection between children, their caregivers, and the special bears they create together. This was the "secret" to creating her successful product, with a vision that was rooted in present-day factors.

MYTH NO. 3: SUCCESS MEANS NEVER GOING BACKWARD

Reality: Yes, successful people are committed to making their vision happen. But they are also willing to change direction.

Jeanne Bice knows this. She realizes that she can't get too attached to any one product, no matter how much she may personally love it.

"A loser is a loser is a loser," said Jeanne. "I don't care if you color it purple and put a pink bow on it, it's a loser and that's a hard lesson to learn. If something isn't selling, put it on sale and get rid of your losses."

Rachel Ashwell also understands the need to change and evolve. She's just entered another stage of her business, accepting funding from venture capitalists to help take the company to the next level.

"In order to grow the business to the next stage I recognized I needed two things: the need to attain significant capital and to attract an experienced executive team with a proven track record of achieving this kind of growth," says Rachel.

MYTH NO. 4: ONLY RISK BRINGS REWARDS

Reality: Any entrepreneurial venture involves some risk, yes. But you don't have to risk everything in order to find success.

Almost every one of the Millionaire Moms took great pains to minimize their risks. Whether it was growing "organically" by using only company revenue to grow, like Teri Gault, or maintaining a manageable pace of growth, like Kathy Gendel, none of the women would consider themselves extremists when it comes to risk-taking.

"Our philosophy is 'slow and steady wins the race,'" said Kathy. "We've never tried to grow too quickly."

MYTH NO. 5: YOUR #1 PRIORITY HAS TO BE MONEY

Reality: For many entrepreneurs, millionaire status is a by-product of their original goals. In my own case, it was never the money alone that motivated me to build Mom Inventors, Inc. And a number of the Millionaire Moms are still stunned that they turned their kitchen-table businesses into multi-million dollar ventures.

Victoria Knight-McDowell, who created the phenomenally successful Airborne, was surprised by the rate of her success. "We never expected it to get this big," Victoria says. "It just absolutely took on a life of its own."

Jeanne Bice also values other aspects of running a business. "Not every business is for a financial reward," she shares. "If you aren't making a wonderful living at it, you're not in the right place."

Terrie Williams puts it this way. "If you don't get up in the morning with butterflies in your stomach, it means you're either going through life being pathetic or you're flat-lining. Because the butterflies, as horrible as they feel, mean that you're challenging yourself and taking your game to the next level."

So now that we've explained what it *doesn't* take to helm a successful business, let's explore more about what it *does* take.

WHAT DOES IT TAKE?

From my own experience, and from the many insights shared by our Millionaire Moms, I've found that there are four essential parts to answering the question, "What does it take to be successful?"

- Clarity regarding your life goals
- An understanding of what you seek to build
- Insight about the traits successful business leaders possess
- Flexibility and the will to do whatever it takes

In the following sections I will explain each of these concepts further.

KNOWING YOUR LIFE GOALS

In Chapter 2, we discussed the importance of writing and verbalizing your Living Dream. Now that we are near the end of the book, this step remains just as relevant. If your Living Dream is still unclear to you, I hope you will give yourself a gift and take the time to spell it out.

On the other hand, you may have read this book only to decide that starting your own business is not the direction for you. That's fine, too. Not everyone is meant to start a business. In fact, I would feel that this book is a success if it has given you clarity of direction and purpose, no matter what the outcome. The secret is that no matter what your direction, it should be clear in your own mind, so that you can feel resolved about what you want to do in this life. Otherwise it's easy to drift along, feeling as if *"life is 'happening' to me"* as opposed to *"this is the life I am creating."*

THE INSIDE STORY

Lillian Vernon

Lillian Vernon literally started her business on her kitchen table. In 1951, a newly married housewife expecting her first child, Lillian used $2,000 of her wedding gift money to start a mail order business. She designed a purse and a belt, which could be personalized with her customers' initials—a brand-new concept at the time—and put a $495 ad in *Seventeen* magazine to advertise it. The ad generated $32,000 in orders!

Lillian slowly built on this success. In 1956 she published her first catalog, with 16 black and white pages and an expanded product line that included personalized combs, blazer buttons, collar pins, and cuff links.

In 1970, she achieved her first million-dollar year in sales.

During that decade, under the Nixon administration, Lillian envisioned the possibilities as trade opened with China. She was one of the first businesswomen to travel there, and came back with many products to add to her growing catalogs. This would be a turning point for her company.

"You have to be determined and you have to be committed," said Lillian. "Stay focused, work hard, and try not to give up too much time with your family."

She is the mother of two sons, both of whom worked for the business at various points in their careers.

Today, the company sends out more than 100 million catalogs per year in 22 editions, with more than 293,000 packages shipped in a peak week. Customers can also order products online at www.lillianvernon.com. Since 1951, more than 130 million orders have been shipped.

Again, it is critical that you put your thoughts in writing and express them out loud. Many experts and successful business owners talk about the importance of stating our intention—what we intend to do if we indeed want to make progress in our lives and achieve our life goals. Then, once you've stated your intention, you need to back it with concerted effort and take action.

"My husband and I were relentless," said Victoria Knight-McDowell. She said that an early investor—a businessman who'd successfully invested in many other companies "said that the one thing that separated us from others was our relentlessness. We had obstacles, but we never let them stay in our way."

At the same time, her Living Dream also included maintaining an intimate family environment for the company. She made this goal clear to the people she hired. In fact, her earliest employees were expected to work on company business as well as pitch in with her baby son when necessary—whatever needed to be done.

"It had to work for the family, and then for Airborne," she explained. "I figured if they had everything in place to be around a family, we could train them to do the other stuff."

Jeanne Bice also understands the importance of visualizing and communicating what you want. "I'm not a woman who should have succeeded, but I had a dream and that's what it takes," Jeanne concurs. "I ask people who come to me, 'What is your dream?' You have to have a burning desire in the pit of your stomach to accomplish something."

You then need to translate this "burning desire" into doing whatever it takes to bring your dream to fruition, even when it gets incredibly difficult and challenging.

Even those entrepreneurs who say their success was *accidental* are not giving themselves enough credit. While early success can be accidental, success at the multi-million dollar level is not. It takes deliberate effort at some point—a lot of hard work, perseverance, passion, and relentless focus. These characteristics and efforts are *not* accidental.

In Julie Garella's book, *Capitalize on Your Success: The Ultimate Guide to Getting the Money, Growing the Business, and Doing the Deal*, she said, "What is stunning to me is that no matter which city I'm in—Boston, Dallas, New York, Hartford, or Raleigh—I always hear the same answers. When asked how they came to be business owners, the universal answer is '*by accident.*' Almost always businesses are started due to a change in the owner's personal life, such as a job loss, parenthood, divorce, or the illness or death of a parent or spouse."

Julie Garella's findings are consistent with my own story and the stories of many of the women entrepreneurs interviewed for this book—in that many of us initiated our businesses as a result of a life circumstance.

UNDERSTANDING WHAT YOU SEEK TO BUILD

Knowing and speaking your Living Dream will help you "lead" your life as opposed to conducting your life in an unplanned or accidental manner. Many of our Millionaire Moms didn't have a specific plan when they began. They built and grew their companies as they went along, as opposed to planning what they wanted from the beginning. But those who didn't have a specific plan now look back and recognize that they would have accomplished more, more quickly, had they better understood what they were building.

Women in particular have varying motivations for becoming entrepreneurs. Some do it because they want to find an outlet for their creativity that's lacking in their personal lives or their current work environment. Some do it to provide a more flexible lifestyle—one that gives them more time with their children. Still others do it to create wealth or to satisfy a vision. Whatever your motivation, it's helpful to understand it clearly in advance. The mom who wants simply to run a part-time business (and keep it that way) will require a different style of leadership than the mom who wants to build an international business.

MILLION-DOLLAR SECRET

"Building a business starts with a passel of emotions—passion, ambition, a sense of accomplishment, a desire to create something special," writes Julie Garella. *"But once you're off and running, the danger of letting emotions rule in the strategic world of business is a key flaw that inhibits many entrepreneurs from creating wealth and achieving true financial security."* (From Capitalize on Your Success: The Ultimate Guide to Getting the Money, Growing the Business, and Doing the Deal by Julie Garella)

LIFESTYLE MAKER OR EMPIRE BUILDER?

In her book, *Capitalize on Your Success*, Julie Garella defines this difference by naming two categories of entrepreneurs: "Lifestyle Makers" and "Empire Builders."

- **Lifestyle Maker.** According to Julie, the Lifestyle Maker wants to have enough money to live comfortably, to be visible as a community business leader, and to be involved in charity, church, or to give back in some way. She develops her company to support a lifestyle. The lines between business and personal life are often blurred.
- **Empire Builder.** Empire Builders have all the above goals, but to a greater extreme. They wish to maximize all the hard work, energy, and resources available to them. They understand how to leverage contacts, resources, and skills to work their plan and build their businesses to the highest level. Many may have started their companies out of circumstance, much like a Lifestyle Maker, but they have a strategy and a plan that they work toward. They also understand how to create wealth, even if it's a by-product of success rather than the initial purpose of the business.

In other words, the Empire Builder is creating the business as a means to an end, whereas the Lifestyle Maker identifies personally with her business and it becomes an extension of her.

"Whether you are a Lifestyle Maker or an Empire Builder, chances are you started out like all successful entrepreneurs—with a good idea and lots of energy," Julie explains in her book. "As your company has grown or matured, you have found yourself at certain forks in the road. The personal and emotional factors that go into making the decisions at these moments are what determine into which category you fall."

When I first read about these two different CEO styles, a light bulb went on. I had observed these two styles over and over, but never pinpointed the difference myself. I also realized that it would be helpful for women to understand their own style and motivation from the outset, in order to create a business that would embody their Living Dream.

For instance, Madelyn Alfano is clearly a Lifestyle Maker. She and her business are firmly intertwined, she is a well-known and well-respected businesswoman in her community, and she loves the lifestyle of running her restaurants. With staff she treats like family (and some family members on staff!), for Madelyn, business and personal are intertwined. This is the fulfillment of Madelyn's Living Dream.

Jeanne Bice, too, is the living embodiment of her company and her products. As the QVC spokesperson for her clothing label, The Quacker Factory, it would be difficult to separate the personal from business even if she wanted to. But she doesn't—she loves what she does and has an exuberance that draws her loyal customers to her.

"People say, 'take a vacation,'" says Jeanne. "Well, I've traveled, I've seen the world, I don't want to go look at a museum in Italy anymore. I love what I'm doing—it's like one great, big, huge party for me, and I'd do it 24 hours a day."

Victoria Knight-McDowell, on the other hand, viewed her company's success as a means to an end—she built her Airborne "empire" not only to provide a product on the market that genuinely helps people but also to create freedom for her family. After intensely building the business, she sold a piece of it and handed over the executive reins to an invest-ment group who shared her vision. While she still remains a significant shareholder, she no longer runs the day-to-day operations. This suits her perfectly—she now has the time to take art classes, take up yoga, and volunteer at her son's ele-mentary school—activities she's always fantasized about hav-ing the time to do. Meanwhile, her husband and partner in the business, a writer by trade, is fulfilling his lifelong dream of making a movie.

"Money allows two things," Victoria says, "freedom and generosity. And both of those things have been the biggest gifts. It's not more material goods." By building this empire and separating from it, her family achieved their own version of a Living Dream.

Julie Clark of Baby Einstein had a similar experience. She never imagined that her videos for babies would take off the way they did—she created them, initially, to fill a need she had with her own children. When the business began to grow at such a rapid rate, she says, it even became over-whelming at times. Even though she felt passionate about her products and helping others, she did not want the permanent lifestyle of CEO—she feared it was taking too much time from her children. This led her to sell the company to Disney. And even though she launched a new company, The Safe Side, she hired trusted professionals to run the day-to-day operations.

"Getting people to reach their potential—it's amazing to me," says Terrie Williams with great excitement. "There are two young people in the past month that I've helped launch a business because they were scared. They are bril-liant! I mean one of them is just a master wordsmith, and that she never thought that she could do it for a living is shocking."

So, it's clear that the women I interviewed identify with these entrepreneurial styles. Although Rachel Ashwell sees herself as a Lifestyle Maker, she is in the process of growing Shabby Chic to the next level. She recently struck a deal with investors that felt right to her. She has maintained the majority ownership of the company, yet the VCs will help her open up 50 new stores over the next few years. This may appear to be building an empire, but it will actually give Rachel more time to spend on the creative side of her business—designing. And while the new partnership will help her company grow, she can maintain her role as a Lifestyle Maker.

WHAT MAKES A MILLIONAIRE MOM?

It's always fascinating to me to find the common thread to any type of success. What makes a good mom? A good friend? A great entertainer, or lawyer, or teacher? That's why I wanted to explore what traits, behaviors, or circumstances these women shared. Are there intangible factors that helped lead to their success? What are their "external" traits (their life circumstances such as where they live, how many children they have, and whether they are married)? And more importantly, what are their "internal" traits? Are they especially inspired or creative? Were they born with something different than others? As I mentioned earlier in the book, my mother frequently told me that "comparison is a killer"—that it can lead to negative feelings about ourselves, and doesn't take into account an individual's complex set of circumstances or complicated nature. Therefore, my search for the common threads among these Millionaire Moms was done with humility—not to "diagnose" and discourage, but rather to inspire! I hope to offer useful information to create a more detailed picture of the realities of becoming a successful entrepreneur.

Terrie Williams

Terrie Williams began her career as a social worker in New York City after earning her Masters Degree from Columbia University. But she always knew she wanted to run her own business. So in 1988, she launched The Terrie Williams Agency, a public relations firm with superstar Eddie Murphy and jazz legend Miles Davis as her first clients.

Her agency quickly became one of the country's most successful public relations and communications firms, with clients including Janet Jackson, Sean "P. Diddy" Combs, Johnnie Cochran, Jackie Joyner-Kersee, Sally Jessy Raphael, Time Warner, HBO, and AT&T—to name just a few. The agency's accomplishments have been used as the basis for public relations seminars and college classes, and Williams is quoted and featured in college textbooks, industry newsletters, and even novels.

Williams is also a successful author and sought-after speaker. Her books include *The Personal Touch: What You Really Need to Succeed in Today's Fast-paced Business World*, a perennial business bestseller. *Stay Strong: Simple Life Lessons for Teens* has been used in school curricula and was the catalyst to launch The Stay Strong Foundation, a national nonprofit that supports America's youth by providing educational resources and mentoring. It has been honored by The National Center for Black Philanthropy with its Special Achievement in Philanthropy Award. *A Plentiful Harvest: Creating Balance and Harmony Through the Seven Living Virtues* is her undertaking to help others achieve balance in their daily lives, reconnect with their heritage, and identify the needs of their souls. Terrie's current work, *Black Pain: It Just Looks Like We're Not Hurting*, will be published in 2007. It tells the untold story of depression among African-Americans, as well as Terrie's tale of her own chronic and crippling depression—a revealing narrative she shared in the June 2005 issue of *ESSENCE* magazine.

To commemorate the tenth anniversary of The Terrie Williams Agency in 1998, Williams donated her collection of business and personal papers to Howard University's Moorland-Spingarn Research Center. The donation was the center's first gift of material specific to the public relations field. Moorland-Spingarn Research Center is the world's largest, most comprehensive repository of information and materials about and by people of African descent, housing works by such legendary figures as Phillis Wheatley, Frederick Douglass, W.E.B. DuBois, Alice Walker, James Baldwin, and Toni Morrison.

Her 28-year-old son, Rocky, is passionate about making a difference in the lives of others.

© Photo credit: Barron Claiborne

"External" Circumstances

On the surface, our Millionaire Moms are very different. They don't all come from privileged backgrounds, nor do they all hail from desperate circumstances. They all come from different backgrounds. They are from all parts of the country. Some are married, some not. Some have a great deal of support from extended families, while others have had to find that support elsewhere. Several of the moms felt that the partnership with their spouses was critical to their success.

Some had educations that ended with high school and others have college and higher degrees. While I didn't specifically ask about this, nothing about their politics or religion seemed obviously similar. Although most of them had one to three children, this is where the commonalities end.

It is when we carefully review the *internal* traits of these women that the obvious connecting thread appears.

"Internal" Traits

There are striking commonalities among the women's internal traits. While they do not share the same outward personalities (some are outgoing and some more introspective, some more high energy and others more laid-back, when we dig deeper we find that there is much more to the story. They are *all* driven. They *all* have a "passion" for what they are doing. And they *all* share an intense determination to succeed at their creation (wherever their creations lead them).

"The secret to my success? Tenacity. Just passion," said Mary Micucci of Along Came Mary Productions. "I have always been passionate about this. You have the business side of it, you have the creative side of it . . . I mean what could be better? What could be more exciting?"

MILLION-DOLLAR SECRET

"One of the things that supposedly holds women back is that we're so emotional, that we want everybody to like us," shares Maxine Clark. "Well, what's so wrong about that? If people like you and trust you and depend on you, they're going to work with you and stay working with you and probably feel really great about working for you. We're finding that those are important skills—and not just necessary for women to have."

These women share a boldness *without arrogance*. Across the board, they work hard, and continue to work hard as their businesses have grown to more complex levels. Even those women who sold their companies have generally continued to work, starting and building new ventures, or throwing themselves into philanthropic work: mentoring, teaching, volunteering, and setting up foundations. They view problems and challenges as opportunities, not obstacles. The word "No" is not an answer that resonates well with them.

When she started Discovery Toys, Lane Nemeth didn't let adversity stand in her way. "The first toy I imported was a total and complete failure," said Lane. "But it didn't stop me."

She went on to encounter countless more obstacles—many much more serious, like a failed computer system in critical weeks leading up to the holidays, as well as near financial ruin—situations she explained in detail in Chapter 7. Although any of these might have led someone else to give up, she persevered.

Victoria Knight-McDowell said the key to her success was not taking anything at face value. Whenever she encountered what seemed to be an insurmountable obstacle, it often ended up working to her company's benefit.

"Work with a problem and see where it takes you," says Victoria. "Every single time we found a better solution, or got some unexpected gift from it."

She shared a story about the challenges of getting a much-needed loan for the company, early on. Although the business was growing strong, she lacked any personal collateral, and it looked like that would be a deal breaker. Then, out of the blue, a woman approached her who loved the product and wanted to invest—but didn't have any money. She did, however, own a condominium—just the collateral Victoria needed for her loan! This "angel" investor has since had a fabulous return on her investment, so everyone has benefited.

Victoria talks about being invited to appear on *Oprah* during the early stages of the business. She made the painstaking decision to turn down the request, because she felt her product just wasn't the right fit for the show topic (folk remedies). Five years later, though, she was invited back. This time it was a perfect fit, and she was in a much better position to handle the huge surge in business after appearing on the show.

Among these women, there is a common belief that there is *always* a way. They also share the ability to be flexible and creative.

When Teri Gault's Web site disappeared into thin air, she found a way to overcome the challenge. When corporate behemoth Jell-O entered the market to compete with Maria Sobrino's premade gelatins, she found a way to thrive. When Debi Davis went bankrupt, she started anew and built a $45 million business. And when former employees of Karen Belasco and Julie Clark, started their own competing companies, they overcame these betrayals. They all found ways to be flexible, creative, and not let adversity get them down.

"I don't think I'm any smarter than anybody else, I don't think I'm particularly more clever—but what I do have is an unwillingness to give up," says Tomima Edmark.

COMMON TRAITS IN OUR MILLIONAIRE MOMS

- Intense focus and determination
- Ability to overcome fear and live boldly
- Ability to look at problems as opportunities
- Belief in something larger than themselves
- Hard work ethic (18-hour work days are common)
- Belief and conviction that they will succeed
- Internal drive
- Flexibility
- Ability to make decisions (even if they aren't always the right ones)
- Passion

The importance of hard work cannot be overstated. In his well-researched article in *Fortune* magazine titled, "What It Takes to Be Great," Geoffrey Colvin wrote:

"You are not a born CEO or investor or chess grand master. You will achieve greatness only through an enormous amount of hard work over many years."

Then, summarizing a body of scientifically examined comparative data, he says, "The first major conclusion is that nobody is great without work. It's nice to believe that if you find the field where you're naturally gifted, you'll be great from day one, but it doesn't happen."

So we can gain both comfort and concern (depending on our frame of mind) from this research. This shows that anyone can achieve greatness regardless of where we start. However, unless we're willing to work hard, it cannot be achieved. He concludes by saying, "Maybe we can't expect most people to achieve greatness—it's just too demanding. But the striking, liberating news is that greatness isn't reserved for a preordained few. It is available to you and to everyone."

PUTTING IT TO WORK FOR YOU

Now that we've defined some of the traits of these successful business-moms, it's important to talk about how you can nurture these traits in yourself.

The first step is to tap into the inspiration and strength within you. That inspiration and strength may come from outside sources—as with these successful women themselves. They may come from a personal role model. They may come from a personal challenge you've had to overcome.

"Listen to your inner voice. Try really hard to fine-tune the ability to listen to your inner voice. It just always tells you what to do. And stay strong and have faith. As I said, I believe in putting God first. And I don't always do it, but He is the reason I am still standing," says Terrie Williams.

Jeanne Bice found strength and will when her husband unexpect-edly died. Madelyn Alfano was inspired by her disabled son's courage and bravery as he fought throughout his life. For me, a near fatal car accident when I was 18 vividly brought my life's direction into focus and has given me a life-long drive to succeed that hasn't diminished over time.

That said, I don't believe that a near-death experience or loss is essential to attaining success. I do believe in everyone's ability to decide to take a new direction, and have witnessed it many times in the course of working with women.

The driving forces varied widely. In some cases, financial con-cerns inspired them to find the will. Debi Davis had little more than a watch to pawn when she started Fit America. Mother of two, Teri Gault was working three jobs when she realized something had to give. And Rachel Ashwell was newly separated from her husband with two small children when she started Shabby Chic. In their cases, necessity prompted them to take action.

For others, their entrepreneurism is driven by a desire to show others that they have the ability to succeed. Even at her lowest point, Maria Sobrino would not give up because she felt the need to prove herself to family back in Mexico. For others, discovering and creating something larger than themselves is what drives them to succeed (in Julie Clark's life, it is the desire to help keep children safe from pred-ators with The Safe Side). Still others may find spiritual inspiration as their guide.

No matter what inspires it, you can find the will to succeed if you aggressively pursue it. It may involve small but important steps like changing your thought and speech patterns. Statements like, "It would sure be nice if . . . " must be replaced with, "It will be great when . . . "

In addition, remembering that achieving your dreams is a choice, not an accident, is a critical part of finding success. Only you can create it.

After the incredible success of TopsyTail, Tomima Edmark wasn't content to rest on her laurels. Part of her reason for starting another company was proving that she wasn't a "one-hit wonder," as she described it. "It bothered me that people would think 'oh, she got lucky.' Because I hate being dismissed for all my hard work." And it wasn't luck that created her success the second time, either.

Again, this doesn't mean you need to go it alone—everyone can benefit from the support of others. But you still must be your own "first investor"—believing in yourself and your idea. Your passion, creativity, and drive will bring others to you.

Although aspects of entrepreneurship can be lonely at times because you are creating something from scratch that at first others may not see or understand, it can be enormously empowering as others eventually join you and believe in you and become a part of what you are creating. Maria Sobrino mentioned the moment of awe she felt as she stood at the door of her factory, watching hundreds of employees and machines producing the millions of desserts she shipped throughout the country each year; she still remembers her humble beginnings, making batches by hand in her small Los Angeles kitchen, delivering them herself to mom-and-pop stores.

THE INSIDE STORY

Deann Murphy

Deann Murphy is a great example of someone who "made lemonade from lemons." In 1972, the Columbia University research center in which she worked suddenly shut down, and she found herself without a job. With extra time on her hands, she was at home with a girlfriend one day, making a quilt for a friend about to have a baby. As they sat there sewing, they got to talking about how others would love to make quilts, too—but that they were time-consuming and challenging to produce. Why not make quilt kits to make it easier for others to create these beautiful heirloom pieces?

That's exactly what they did—developed a quilt kit and sold it to stores like Bloomingdales and Macy's. The kits were an instant hit, garnering coverage in *Good Housekeeping* magazine and selling out quickly. Working from home as a mother to two school-age children, Deann expanded the business over the next 25 years, marketing additional craft products like the Yarn Crafter, Sequin Art, and the BeDazzler, and a world of products to support them. She grew the company into a multi-million dollar business, selling it in 1997.

Today she helps others who'd like to follow in her footsteps, chairing the Women's Business Development Center in Stamford, Connecticut. There she trains and mentors aspiring women entrepreneurs, most of whom are disadvantaged. In addition, she is an active board member of The Center for Women's Business Research, which provides the research knowledge that propels the growth of women business owners and their enterprises to economic and social significance. She is also vice chair of Silver Hill Hospital, and a grandmother to seven children.

© Photo credit: Rose Mettlen

YOUR OWN DREAM

As mothers, women, companions, professionals, entrepreneurs, and more, our lives are complex. This complexity can be difficult to handle, but also can be exhilarating and gratifying. By defining our Living Dream, tackling challenges such as our fears of money, seeking balance, loving our families, learning the fundamentals of building and growing a business, and finally accepting the challenge to do whatever it takes to create the life you want—you too, can find success.

I have shared a few of my own lessons learned in building my business, and the women interviewed for this book have truly laid a path for us to follow. They have also demonstrated that there is nothing preventing us from creating the life we want. It is simply up to you to take the chances necessary to achieve your dreams. My mother always told me: "Leap and the net will appear." I invite you to take that leap.

Index

About the Author

In the spring of 2003, Tamara Monosoff founded her company, Mom Inventors, Inc., where she serves as CEO. The company has the dual mission of manufacturing quality products invented by moms and providing an online community for aspiring women entrepreneurs at www.mominventors.com. Products bearing the Mom Invented® brand can be found in stores and catalogs throughout the United States, United Kingdom, and Australia.

Tamara has appeared on most national television networks including CNN, NBC, CBS, and ABC, as well as dozens of local television and radio shows across the country. She has been featured on the front page of the *Wall Street Journal*, in the *New York Times*, *The Chicago Tribune*, *The London Times*, and *The Financial Times*, as well as *People*, *New Yorker*, *Fortune Small Business*, and *Working Mother* magazines. She is an expert columnist for Entrepreneur.com, and is a frequent speaker on subjects of entrepreneurship and leadership for women. She is also a regular guest on QVC where she markets several of her company's products.

Prior to both motherhood and launching Mom Inventors, Inc., Tamara served as an appointee to the Clinton Administration in both the White House and in the U.S. Department of Education. Her progressive assignments included the position as Senior Communications Associate for the President's Initiative on Race at the White House, Education Director for the President's Commission on White House Fellowships, and Chief of Staff for the Office of Vocational and Adult Education at the U.S. Department of Education.

Following her three-year term in Washington, Tamara lived in Hong Kong for 18 months, where she consulted to American companies entering Asian markets, and spoke on the subject of women and leadership to such groups as the Hong Kong government's Commission on Equal Opportunities and the American Chamber of Commerce. Tamara holds a Master's degree in Psychology and a doctorate in International and Multicultural Education with a dissertation on women in leadership both from the University of San Francisco.

Tamara lives in California where she runs her business with husband and partner, Brad Kofoed. They have two energetic children, five-year-old Sophia Colette, and three-year-old Kiara Lauren.

About Mom Inventors, Inc.

Mom Inventors, Inc. produces and distributes products made by and for moms nationwide. Each product carries the Mom Invented® brand, symbolizing the dynamic creativity of moms everywhere and our potential connection to each other. In the process of building this business, an exciting community has emerged.

The Mom Inventors community is growing exponentially each day. Whether you are developing the next new software application, a new product or service business, or have an inspired idea, this Web site is intended to provide a supportive environment. As a community of "moms helping moms," you'll find informational resources, a message board, seminars, inspiring stories from our featured moms, a newsletter, and our popular Mom Invented™ Store.

We seek to nurture what mothers do best—solve problems—and in so doing change the rules by which we live. There are 82 million moms in the United States. We represent the largest source of untapped entrepreneurial intelligence in this country. Mom Inventors has recognized these untapped resources and uncovered a widespread urge to create. Through collaboration and by leveraging our hard-earned wisdom and stamina, each of us can design the lives we seek and ultimately change society in ways not yet imagined.

I invite you to join our community and to take action and the chances necessary to achieve your dreams. Please begin now by visiting our Web site at www.mominventors.com/millionairemoms. Remember, "Leap and the net will appear."

Special Invitation

In Chapter 2, I talk about the importance of stating your intention. And throughout the book, many of the Millionaire Moms talk about the value of seeking out mentors and supportive networks.

This is why I've organized all the resources mentioned in the book into one easy place for you to access at our online community. I invite you to join our community by visiting www.mominventors.com/millionairemoms. Whether you want to change your life, make a million dollars, or support others, you'll find access to all the resources mentioned in the book, plus additional interactive resources such as message boards, downloads, and our monthly newsletter.

I invite you to become a member of our active and supportive community today!